BAR-H
Ruth Bro
Marie Stringer
Elizabeth Ellis
Jonnye Butler

The Long Good Night

The Long Good Night

MY FATHER'S JOURNEY
INTO ALZHEIMER'S

Daphne Simpkins

William B. Eerdmans Publishing Company

Grand Rapids, Michigan / Cambridge, U.K.

© 2003 Wm. B. Eerdmans Publishing Co.
All rights reserved

Wm. B. Eerdmans Publishing Co.
255 Jefferson Ave. S.E., Grand Rapids, Michigan 49503 /
P.O. Box 163, Cambridge CB3 9PU U.K.

Printed in the United States of America

08 07 06 05 04 03   7 6 5 4 3 2 1

ISBN 0-8028-3971-1

www.eerdmans.com

For Daddy's bodyguards with love and admiration:

Kathryn Ellen Simpkins

Julie Ann Simpkins Helms

Patricia Cathryn Simpkins

Mary Ellen McCord

Dr. Guin Splawn Nance

And in memory of the woman whose prayers
helped to sustain us all:

Esther Floyd Splawn
February 17, 1916–March 8, 1999

Contents

PROLOGUE: Magnificent Edifice   x

I HEARTLAND

1 His Number-One Helper   3

From the Family Album . . .
My Most Unforgettable Character   12

2 The Look of Love   17

From the Family Album . . .
Dad Goes Bananas   24

3 The Midas Touch   27

From the Family Album . . .
The Midnight Shift   35

II FAMILY LAND

4 The Dream House   43

From the Family Album . . .
The Legacy of a Very Handy Man   51

vii

5 Private Road   54

   From the Family Album . . .

      An Evening Sky   60

6 Can You Hear Me, Brother Woodrow?   62

   From the Family Album . . .

      Across the Creek from Luckytown   66

7 A Stolen Life   70

   From the Family Album . . .

      Living on the Flood Plain   75

8 The Mother Load   78

   From the Family Album . . .

      Causes and Effects   85

9 The Sleeping Alligator   90

   From the Family Album . . .

      Sweet Dreams of a Cruise   96

III WILDERNESS

10 A Disappearing Act   105

   From the Family Album . . .

      Say Good-bye   110

11 Just the Facts   114

   From the Family Album . . .

      My Mother's Child   122

12 Those Gray Areas   124

   From the Family Album . . .

      James Bond, Mr. Coffee, and Dr. No   130

13 Good Girls Gone Bad   133

   From the Family Album . . .
      Prisoner of Love   139

14 Cain's Chapel   142

   From the Family Album . . .
      When Sofas Curse   147

15 Morning Has Broken   150

   From the Family Album . . .
      The Close Shave   154

16 Life at The Rock   157

   From the Family Album . . .
      Confabulation!   162

IV HEAVENLY PLACES

17 Tell Me a Story   169

   From the Family Album . . .
      Resurrection   177

18 Party Girl   180

   From the Family Album . . .
      An Angel's Kiss   189

19 God Is Love   192

   From the Family Album . . .
      Death Takes Its Time   198

   EPILOGUE: The Appraisal   201

   From the Family Album . . .
      Babe in the Woods   205

Acknowledgments   208

PROLOGUE

Magnificent Edifice

"That is a magnificent edifice," Daddy commented as we drove past the newest addition to the Methodist church.

"It is," I replied.

Like so many casual observations, the two words Daddy spoke were not only a commentary about the Methodists' very grand building but also a little test he was giving himself in front of me.

Daddy was sick, the doctors said, and we had been warned that one of the clues that death was winning out over life would be when his language skills began to slip. If he could still say *magnificent edifice*, he was okay. We grinned happily at each other as I came to a stop at the five-way intersection where I've done a lot of my praying.

I'm not alone. Many people stop at this dangerous intersection and whisper a prayer for a safe crossing. "Lord, help us," I prayed silently.

It was sufficient to call upon God's very present grace, and almost immediately, I needed it. A sudden film descended over Daddy's gaze as I crossed the intersection and steered toward Main Street. He blinked rapidly, fidgeted with his seat belt, and suddenly opened his car door. Unaware that he was in danger of falling out of a moving vehicle, Daddy grinned at me as if he'd done something very clever.

My right hand reached out and gripped his arm as I slowed the car. Heart racing, grin now frozen on my face, I steered into the parking lot of the local park. I turned off the engine, pocketed the keys, and went around to my daddy's door, where I secured his seat belt once more. He eyed me curiously, as if he didn't recognize me. I smiled, and something inside of him clicked. He smiled back. I kissed his cheek, got back in the car, and this time flipped the child-protection lock so that he couldn't open the door again.

Easing back onto Main Street, I mentally crossed off two of the errands I needed to run and asked him if he was hungry.

"I can always eat a little something," he replied good-naturedly.

He had the same insatiable appetite that my grandmother developed when she slipped into dementia of the Alzheimer's variety. That's what doctors called Daddy's disease. They said it was the constant roaming that fed the appetite: "He's hungry because he burns off so many calories looking for what he thinks he's lost."

When an Alzheimer's patient tries to answer a question and doesn't use facts, doctors may diagnose the response as a symptom of the disease and name it *confabulation*. In my opinion, some doctors confabulate. That is, some medical practitioners make up causes to explain the effects associated with this mysterious disease. I have nothing against confabulation. To some extent, we all confabulate. We tell stories to record history; we tell stories to fill in the gaps our flawed memories leave; we tell stories to create order out of what feels like the incomprehensible stuff of daily life.

For the past eighteen years, I've written my family's stories for different periodicals, creating what I call a "Family Album" about daily life with Daddy. In the process I have caught snapshots of how Alzheimer's announces itself before and after it is diagnosed. These snapshots are tucked at the end of the narrative chapters of this book, which chronicles the story of a family growing older together.

Some stories about Alzheimer's can confirm certain fears and build others. Fear of the unknown. Fear of losing your own life and not being able to find it again. Fear of the implications of a great unraveling of the mind and a questioning of how faith, will, and human love do not stop this obsolescing from occurring. Questions for caregivers abound in the chaos created by living with someone who has Alzheimer's. It is a state of being that often looks meaningless, but it is not.

There is a redeeming force at work in the process of someone's mind dying faster than his body. The person with the sick mind deteriorates, but for the people around him, the truth sharpens. The complexity of truth's nature is revealed. Joy is still possible, hope viable, and anger and frustration can be changed into laughter and music.

The Long Good Night is as much about living life with Daddy as it is about coming to live more wholly with God as our only perfect Father. He is with us at the various intersections of our lives, on the physical streets where we build our houses, and ultimately, in that mysterious invisible place where our souls dwell. He promised to make his home with us, and he does.

That is the magnificent edifice.

I

HEARTLAND

1

His Number-One Helper

"We're headed out, Lola. Are you going to be here when we get back?"

"Your daddy thinks I'm going to disappear," Mother said without looking up.

She sat cross-legged on the living-room floor in front of the console TV. The morning newspaper was spread out before her as she sipped her first cup of coffee. The television was on, but the volume was low. Perry Mason was still stringing Della Street along while he brought another bad guy to justice.

"Shorty?" Daddy said. Mother was five-foot-two, and Daddy liked to tease her.

"How long are you two going to be gone?" she asked to prove she was listening.

"It's always too long when I'm away from you," Daddy said, crossing the room. He bent over and kissed Mother on the back of her neck.

She shivered with the kiss and looked up at Dad. He was six feet tall and handsome, and she knew it. "Where are you going?"

"We're stopping in on Annie Warren first, and then going over to assess the Russells' house," Daddy said.

"You are sneaking off to see your girlfriend. Is that it?" Mother asked dryly.

"Just that one," Daddy said.

Daddy had been helping Annie Warren keep up her house for

years. She was an aging spinster who had been taking care of her sick daddy for as long as I had known her. Daddy and I usually performed some household repair while Mother visited with her.

"Did you see that story about George Wallace?" Daddy asked. He nudged Mother's hip with his right foot.

"No, I didn't see it," Mother said. Smoke from her Pall Mall drifted over her head. Her soft brown curls caught the light.

"It was on the front page," Daddy declared, feigning exasperation. "I don't know how you can call yourself reading the newspaper and not see a story on the front page."

"George needs to try and keep himself off the front page," Mother said, as Daddy dropped to a stoop beside her. His posture remained perfect. He was fifty-four years old, but he could hold that pose for as long as he needed to.

Mother's large brown eyes were magnified behind her reading glasses, making her look younger than her forty-nine years. Daddy lost himself in Mother's gaze for a moment, and I finally gave up and sat back down to wait until they finished saying good-bye. I had unusual parents. After thirty-two years of marriage, they were still in love. Even leaving the house to run a couple of errands was an occasion to pitch a little woo.

"Don't mind me," I said, as my gaze drifted to the senior portraits of my three sisters and me on the wall where they were hung in the shape of a diamond. My oldest sister's picture was on top. Mary Ellen's black hair was in a perfect, saucy flip. She was two years older than I, and a deep intelligence emanated from her large hazel eyes. Patty Kate's picture was on the right. A year younger than I, Patty Kate was the pretty one, thin and feminine with light blue eyes and chestnut hair that belonged to a princess — Daddy's nickname for her.

To the left was Julie Ann's picture. Long, wavy auburn hair tumbled to her shoulders. Forest-green eyes seemed trained on the horizon. The baby of the family, Julie Ann looked like Joan of Arc to me, valiant and pure-hearted. She was the last to graduate high school six years ago.

My picture was below Mary Ellen's. I had brown eyes and red hair like Daddy's. Although I wore the traditional white cloud wrap off the shoulders, that softening effect did not disguise my bookish demeanor. My eyes did my smiling for me. I looked like I had a secret, but I was mostly an open book — I was the unmarried daughter who, at twenty-eight, still lived at home.

"Who cares about Wallace?" Daddy was saying. "It's you and me, Shorty. You going to get dressed any time soon? I could take you out to lunch when I get back."

"Is this a date, or do you have some land you want to look at, Jerry?" Mother asked.

"It could be both," Daddy said, his voice changing. "When you get to the classifieds, you'll see an ad for fifty acres in Autauga County." He reached toward the newspaper to show Mother the ad. When she slapped at his hand, he grinned as if she'd kissed him.

"If it has good road access and can pass a perc test, I could buy it and subdivide it into five-acre tracts. I think most people want a little piece of land. And that's where the money is. Selling a house is just a one-time profit, but selling lots and financing it yourself means you collect the interest."

Mother looked past Daddy. His scuffed, burnt-orange briefcase was already parked by the front door. He had bought it years ago when he began selling insurance, but those days were over. Now it was filled with sales contracts and a map of the state for his expeditions to investigate land for sale. He had been looking for a parcel of land for about a year, since he had retired as a civil engineer from Maxwell Air Force Base. At first he had been at loose ends and had started following Mother around the house all day while she did her chores.

Mother had finally snapped one day and said, "Jerry, find something to do!"

That was when Daddy had begun to think about buying and selling land.

"Autauga County is big. How far is far?" Mother asked.

"What do you care, if you're sitting in the car with me?" Daddy placed his hand on her back and smoothed a wrinkle in Mother's yellow robe. Her eyes softened at his touch, and her body leaned into his.

"Jim's Restaurant is on the way back, and I could buy you some fried chicken for lunch. You too, Daffodil," he offered.

I didn't decline immediately, but I would. Two was company on that kind of drive; three was a crowd.

"Does that offer of lunch include lemon ice-box pie?" Mother asked, tilting her head.

"Maybe," he replied. "Depends on how nice you are to me in the car."

"I can be pretty nice," Mother flirted back. "I'll be dressed by the time you get back," she promised, folding the page in the newspaper with the crossword puzzle and the Jumble on it. No one else touched that page of puzzles. It was her daily treat. She loved words; we had that in common.

"Hold down the fort," Daddy said, as he finally opened the front door.

"Don't I always?" she replied archly.

He laughed in response and stepped back so that I could precede him, then strode past me to open the passenger door of his gold Cadillac for me. As he walked around to the driver's side, his curly red hair caught the sun, a vivid contrast to his unusual eyes: one blue, one green. He was blind in the green one.

"What are we doing at Miss Annie's today?" I asked. I hoped it wasn't anything too complicated. I was due at my job at the newspaper at one o'clock.

"Stopped-up kitchen sink. Miss Annie pours grease down her sink. I've warned her over and over, but she just doesn't understand why grease won't wash through. Sometimes I think she does it to give herself a reason to call some company to come over."

Not just any company. Daddy.

"I've told her to fill up the sink once a week with scalding hot water and soap and let it drain in a big rush. . . ." I tuned out the rest of Daddy's instructions on how to keep a sink in running order. I could have said the words for him. There wasn't much about home maintenance that Daddy hadn't shared with me through the years. He was an expert handyman, and I was his number-one helper.

We took the familiar right turn to Miss Annie's house and parked in her driveway. Miss Annie opened the front door before we had a chance to ring the bell. She looked pale, and her dark hair was laced with gray. Her loose, floral cotton housedress was faded from being dried on the clothesline in the sun.

Daddy walked past Miss Annie, leaving the chore of making small talk to me. "Mama says hello," I said. "You're looking awful pretty." It was what Mother always told her.

"How is your mother?" she asked politely.

Before I could answer, she waved a ring-less hand in the direction of her daddy's bedroom. "Papa is sleeping. Come into the parlor," she whispered. Her eyebrows raised, she said, "I've got a little present for you and your daddy."

I didn't have to ask what it was. She disappeared into the kitchen while I took Mother's regular seat in the parlor.

I heard Daddy rustling around in the kitchen, and Miss Annie giggled. He was teasing her about stopping up the sink. I missed being in there with him. When Mother came, I helped Daddy. When she didn't, I kept Miss Annie company.

Miss Annie returned with her pale cheeks pinker and a sparkle in her round, dark eyes. She handed me a spicy cheese log wrapped in wax paper. She had been making these treats for Daddy ever since he said he liked them twenty years ago. Miss Annie sat down across from me and asked what I had been doing.

"Going to college and working at the newspaper part-time," I replied.

"I almost had a job once. What do you do there?" she asked.

"I type," I said, which wasn't the entire truth. I was the obituary clerk. Morticians drove by each afternoon and passed me long sheaves of paper with the names and facts of the newly deceased, and I typed up their life stories for the next day's edition.

"What will you do after you graduate?" she asked.

"Daddy wants me to be a librarian, but I want to write books." I already wrote stories, mostly at night in my journal.

"She's done," Daddy said, joining us quickly. "Just a little grease clog, Miss Annie." He stood beside her chair, and she crossed her legs self-consciously. Her red-rough hand smoothed the hem of her dress as she shifted her body away from him. Miss Annie could only love Daddy from a-far. When he was near, she grew nervous and self-conscious. "We'll be seeing you, Miss Annie. You call us any time," Daddy said. "We're as close as the telephone."

"It's so comforting to know you are nearby . . ." Miss Annie began her litany of thanks as we moved toward the front door.

"Thanks again for the cheese log," I said, as I walked ahead in case she wanted to talk to Daddy privately. Sometimes ladies did. Daddy had been a Sunday school teacher for many years and a back-up preacher for a couple of churches, and ladies often had prayer requests to make of him. I respected that.

I watched from the car. Secure in the doorway with Daddy on his way out, Annie Warren relaxed. Her hand moved girlishly through her salt-and-pepper hair. She tilted her head and smiled up at him. I vowed to myself: *Never let a man see you looking at him like that.*

"She's a sweet old girl," Daddy declared as he took his place behind the steering wheel. "And she seems perfectly happy there with her daddy." Daddy gave me a quick glance to see if I'd heard him. I smiled neutrally. "You know your mother and I make a big thing out of our being in love, but there are many ways to be happy. I can see you as a librarian."

Daddy's advice to me had evolved through the years. He used to tell me, "It's as easy to fall in love with a rich man as a poor one" and "Beware of men in uniforms. They look sharper than they are. Some of them can't even change a lightbulb." But now he mainly talked to me about business. "Learn computers — that's the wave of the future. And get yourself a state job with a good retirement plan." He saw me now as someone who would need to make her own living.

I placed the cheese log on the back seat, and Daddy cranked the Cadillac and backed out onto the street. He looked over his shoulder, not trusting the peripheral vision of his blind eye. We were just a couple of blocks from the Russells' house.

Old friends or acquaintances like the Russells often called Daddy for free advice about how to get a house ready to sell. They thought he had the Midas touch. He did, and I knew what it was.

"Nobody's home," Daddy said as we turned into the driveway of a one-story, brown brick house. I scanned the gray shingles on the roof. A sparrow darted into the chimney carrying a leaf.

"The Russells have already moved out and taken most of their furniture," Daddy said, using the key from underneath the front-door mat. He pushed the door open and waited for me to go first. I stepped into the dark foyer. It felt like a tomb. Instinctively Daddy moved to my side in case I needed protecting. It was that kind of house.

He sighed deeply. "What do you see, Daffodil?"

Daddy often tested my powers of observation the same way he quizzed Mother about the content of the morning newspaper.

"The carpet is very worn," I observed as my eyes adjusted to the ill-lit room.

Daddy walked over to where the carpet met the wall and eased his finger into the seam. He tugged gently and looked at the floor underneath. "Bingo!" he whispered as if to himself. "They could rip up the carpet and refinish these hardwood floors underneath. A good wood floor can sell a house."

I walked over to the swinging door that led to the kitchen. The stove was caked in grease, as was the ventilator. The porcelain sink needed bleaching. The faucet dripped. "I can already tell you what the bathrooms will look like," I said, returning to the living room. "They will need Clorox."

Daddy shook his head. His Midas touch was built on a simple philosophy: A well-maintained house advertises owners who have taken care of the property. *A clean house always sells faster than a dirty one.*

"I'll check the bedrooms," I said.

"Be careful," he responded automatically. It was what he always said when I left him. "I'm going to see if the fireplace works, although why anyone would want a fireplace in Alabama where we don't have any real winter I'll never know."

The bedrooms were empty. The carpet bore the imprint of absent beds and dressers. I checked inside the gloomy closets.

"Where are you?" Daddy called. Mother was right. Daddy often thought one of us was going to disappear.

"Coming," I said.

He was bent down beside the fireplace, struggling with the damper. "I hate this kind of flue. It sits on that notch, and if it isn't caught just right, it gets out of whack." Finally he jerked on the handle, and the flue opened. A few leaves and pine needles floated down.

"I saw a bird building a nest in the chimney when we drove up," I said, gesturing toward the debris.

"Smoke will run them off," he said. "Will you make a note of that?"

I nodded. "They have never painted the inside of the closets," I reported.

Daddy shook his head in wonder. He looked over my head at a crystal chandelier that was covered in cobwebs.

"Windex?" I asked.

He nodded succinctly.

"I'll add it to the list," I said. That was really my job. When Daddy and I inspected a house together, I made a list and typed up all the suggestions for him to give the seller.

"Anything else?" he asked.

"What did I miss?" I replied. He grinned, ready to answer, but just as he did, a strange cloud passed behind his eyes. He reached out to the back of a chair to steady himself. Then he sat down heavily by the lonesome dining-room table that had been left behind.

The experience of time changed then. We moved into slow motion. "Daddy?" I whispered softly, and my words rose up in the air and passed slowly to where he was. He looked blankly down at the floor, his arm braced on the table for support.

"Daddy?" My hand went out and began to reach for him, but it took a long time. Finally I touched his shoulder. He was very still — a statue.

"I'll get you a glass of water," I said. My words echoed in the room. He looked up, and when he did, his eyes were different. He looked like a stranger.

"I'll be right back," I said. His head bobbed gently up and down, and I pretended not to see that.

I found an old milky green glass coffee cup in the kitchen cabinet and filled it from the tap. When I placed it in front of Daddy, the water made a ring on the Russells' good wood table, and I didn't care.

"I'm not really thirsty," he said slowly, ignoring the cup. He tried to smile. "I just felt kind of not like myself."

He was sounding stronger. I took a deep breath. "We're basically finished here. Let's go home," I urged.

"Maybe we better," he agreed. He pushed himself up, unfolding his spine until he was standing again. The light in his eyes began to come back; but just as it did, the sun went behind a cloud, and the room lost its natural light. Daddy's eyes met mine. "I'm not sure I can do it anymore," he whispered.

"Do what anymore?" I asked. He didn't answer me.

"Daddy. Mother is waiting for you," I said. That got his attention.

"You drive," he said, slowly leading the way out the front door. He always held the door for me — but not this time.

I locked it behind us, catching up with him as he got into the passenger seat. I made the bright chitchat that girls raised in the South use to fill awkward silences. We drove three streets down and took a right turn. By the time we reached home, Daddy felt better. And when he got out of the car, he laughed at the look of concern on my face.

"I'm glad you love me that much, but really, there's nothing wrong with me that a good old cup of coffee and an oatmeal cookie won't fix."

He held the front door for me, and I went through it, holding Miss Annie's cheese log. I kissed his cheek quickly as I passed by. It was very cool and redolent of Old Spice cologne. He patted my shoulder as he called out to Mama, just like always, "We're home."

From the Family Album . . .

My Most Unforgettable Character

"Bon jour. Bon soir. C'est moi." I flung a few French phrases over my shoulder as I gathered my books to head to my French class. I had a hard time pronouncing foreign words and attempted to ameliorate my insecurity by saying the words to anyone near me before I actually had to do it in front of Madame Hill and my classmates.

"Bon jour to you too," Daddy replied, rising from his desk, where he had been reading, to walk me to the door. He often did that — escorted me to the door when I was leaving, and then from the doorway he would call a few familiar sayings of his own after me: *Be careful. It's easy to have an accident. One moment of thoughtlessness is enough to ruin the rest of your life.*

Today he didn't warn me about anything. He asked a question instead. "The *Reader's Digest* says that all children have a particular memory of a parent that is theirs alone. Do you have a special memory of me?"

The mantel clock snuffled rather than chimed because Daddy had muffled the bell. We had not liked the clock's noisy reminder that time was passing. This whimpering event was still loud enough to remind me that I had to get to my class.

"I can't think of anything," I replied quickly.

"The *Reader's Digest* says you can," he asserted, moving further out the door. It wasn't that he didn't believe me. It was that he didn't believe that the *Reader's Digest* could ever be wrong.

I shrugged the way a young college woman studying French does when she wants to appear to be living a more adventurous life than she really is. Daddy stood in the doorway, watching me back out of the driveway, and I could feel his mind racing ahead to the challenges of my day. I waved good-bye to him over the steering wheel as the warnings recycled in both of our minds simultaneously: *Be careful at the intersection next to Richardson's Pharmacy. People often try to scoot through that light. Lock your car doors once you're inside. Pay attention to what's going on around you. Check your gas gauge.*

I chose the long way to French class, through the old neighborhood where F. Scott Fitzgerald had courted Zelda. I liked the slow way to most places — a key to my nature that I hid from others the same way I pretended to my family that I was smarter in college than I really was. I was thinking with dread about the day's test when suddenly the steering wheel trembled in my hand. A thumping began. I eased up on the gas. Daddy had been warning me for years that this could happen: I had a flat tire.

"Mon Dieu!" I exclaimed, slowing to the curb.

I opened the trunk, spied the jack and the spare, and I remembered everything Daddy had taught me: I was supposed to pry off the hubcap, jack up the car, twist loose the lug nuts, lift off the flat, and put on the doughnut spare. But all I could do was say out loud, "I can't do that."

Instead, I walked to a nearby house, asked to use the phone of one of those strangers who might kill me, went right on inside where danger lurked, and called Daddy. I told him where I was and what had happened.

I felt his adrenaline rush in response to my call for help. His voice got stronger, and he said, "Get out of that house right now. Go back to the car and wait for me. I'll be right there." I thanked the stranger for the use of the phone and went back to the car to wait for Daddy.

He didn't appear right away, and I grew warm in the morning sun. I was already late to class, and my anxiety about the test intensified when I realized that I would have to take a make-up. Surely that would be harder.

Nervous, I was scanning the far end of the street for Daddy's Cadillac when I saw Daddy jog around the corner and run toward me in his good blue-and-burgundy business suit.

When he saw me, Daddy waved exuberantly. Then, after he knew I was safe, his body relaxed, and he gave himself over to the physicality of running, enjoying his own strength and motion.

I resisted the impulse to run toward him. It was always my impulse, but I was a college girl studying French, after all. Daddy saw me hold back, but he kept running toward me anyway, smiling broadly. When he reached me, he was laughing at himself and with relief that I was all right. "When you called, I got in such a hurry that I locked myself out of the house and my car. I'll need a lift home."

"I couldn't change the tire," I explained. "I know you taught me how, but I don't have the strength in my arms." It was a limp lie. I hadn't even tried.

He waved aside my apology. "As long as one of us can do it, we're all right." It was what he always said when he helped me.

Positioning the crowbar I had retrieved from the trunk, Daddy said, "If you can't reach me the next time you have a flat, use your foot this way to create leverage with the crowbar. Your leg is stronger than your arm. Kick it like this. Of course, girls don't often wear the right kind of shoes for this maneuver." He took his dressy handkerchief out of his suit pocket and wiped his hands on it as if it were an old rag.

I smiled apologetically, a girl wearing the wrong kind of shoes. "You're all dressed up," I acknowledged ruefully. "Am I making you late for an appointment?"

"You could never make me late for anything that matters to me more than you do," he replied.

We worked in silence then. I handed him the tools as he asked for them. It was a familiar pattern. Ever since I had been a little girl, I had been his number-one helper.

He finished the job, putting the flat tire in the trunk and securing the jack so that it wouldn't rattle. "I'll get that flat tire fixed for you," he offered.

"I could take it somewhere," I proposed weakly.

"You can when you don't have me to do it for you," he said.

I nodded my thanks as he got in the passenger seat. It was a short drive home.

I parked in our driveway, and Daddy opened the car door and

looked at me sheepishly. "I need you to unlock the side door to my office."

I followed him on that well-worn path from the car to the side door. Each footstep forward was also a step backward in time. Each step brought a memory. The first kiss from my boyfriend — and the last. The night Mary Ellen came knocking on my window when her son Matthew was about to be born. The countless times I heard Daddy's footsteps crunch the gravel on his way to work the midnight shift at the air force base.

"There are my keys!" Daddy announced when I opened the door. He was relieved that his key ring had not disappeared. Things did that around him sometimes. But there they were, right on top of the *Reader's Digest,* which lay open to the essay he had been reading earlier.

Daddy's still-unanswered question about a signature memory of him rose up between us. Embarrassed that he had asked, Daddy fumbled with the magazine and placed it on the stack of reading materials that he kept to take to hospitals and to people confined at home. It was near the wall map of the state of Alabama and his big green filing cabinet, where he stored all his memorabilia.

I wanted to tell him that I remembered working with him at the old apartment building on Alabama Street that he had renovated, and how we collected the rent together. That I remembered how, when he left to work the midnight shift, he came by my bedroom window and tapped on the glass with his fingertips to tell me good night.

"Is there something else?" Daddy asked as he felt me linger in the shadows of his office. The mantel clock made its muffled sound, and we both looked at it, surprised that it kept trying to proclaim the passing of time with its bell swaddled in cotton.

I pointed toward the *Reader's Digest.* "I'll always remember how you ran toward me in your good suit today — in a hurry to reach me. And you always say, 'As long as one of us can do it, we're all right.' I'll remember that," I promised him.

He smiled curiously, glad and a little embarrassed to think that I had gained my special memory of him only that day. But I hadn't.

He was right before. The *Reader's Digest* was right too.
I remembered my daddy.
I remembered everything.

2

The Look of Love

"Good night, Miss Agnes!" Daddy exclaimed when the lightbulb he was attempting to change broke off in his hand. "Is the switch off?" he asked, as he inspected the shards of glass protruding from the socket. The ladder he was standing on quivered. I reached out and steadied it.

"Believe it is," I replied.

"Hand me the insulated pliers," he directed. I reached into his toolbox and found the pair he meant. Using the pliers, he gripped the side of the bulb's base and began to twist gingerly. "Don't you ever do this," he cautioned me. "If this ever happens to you, call me. I'd like to be the one who gets electrocuted."

"I know," I replied, sighing. Daddy often volunteered to die in my place. And danger was everywhere. Ironically, he had recently been electrocuted at the hospital where I had taken him to get his heart shocked back into a sinus rhythm. After his weak spell at the Russells' house, Daddy had gone in for a physical. They had discovered he had arrhythmia, a condition sometimes treated by pills or electric shock to put the heart back into a regular rhythm.

"I've heard you can take half a potato and push it into the broken shards and use that as a grip to twist out the rest of the bulb. It should work," he mused, twisting slowly. "But lightbulbs really should just go in and come out the way they're supposed to." The broken one finally loose, Daddy looked around for some place to put it other than my naked hand. I picked up the nearby wastebasket, and he tossed it in.

"I need a sixty-watter," he said. "Go any higher, and you're just begging to be burned down. I don't even know why your mother buys the 100-watters. She knows I don't believe in using them."

"Mother likes to live dangerously," I replied.

He installed the new bulb while I spritzed the fixture cover with Windex and wiped it out. *As long as you're changing the bulb, you might as well clean the fixture.* Wordlessly, I handed Daddy the cloth, and he wiped around the base, shining it up.

"It's good to see you doing something useful, Jerry," Uncle Tommy said, suddenly appearing in the doorway. The front door was unlocked, and he had let himself in — like he was supposed to. My heart leapt up. I was always glad to see him.

"A man can't stay in bed forever," Daddy replied, stepping down from his ladder. "You going to put the coffee on?" he asked me. "And you better tell your mother her brother's here."

"The coffee is probably already on. I heard Mother in the kitchen a few minutes ago."

"Good — you're in time to eat," Daddy said.

"I didn't come to eat," Tommy replied. He was a big, handsome man with an easy smile.

"You could eat a little snack," Daddy coaxed as he folded up the stepladder. He leaned it against the door frame until later. There were other lightbulbs that needed changing.

Daddy and Uncle Tommy headed toward the dining-room table, where Mother had placed her butter-almond pound cake, one of Daddy's favorites. I knew it would still be warm — crusty on the outside and tender on the inside. I set Daddy's toolbox by the front door. The TV was on in the living room, as usual. *Pal Joey* was playing. Rita Haworth was in the shower singing "Bewitched, Bothered, and Bewildered." I watched her be in love with Frank Sinatra for a minute — didn't blame her — while Daddy counseled Uncle Tommy about romance and women.

A widower for years, Uncle Tommy had recently reconnected

with Bonnie, his high-school sweetheart, and it looked like love. Since then, Uncle Tommy had been asking Daddy all kinds of questions. Today I eavesdropped while Uncle Tommy asked what a bride would expect in the way of a honeymoon.

Daddy was supposed to know. My parents had been honeymooning for years. Whenever one of the cable channels ran a James Bond marathon, they drove thirty miles up the road to a motel in Clanton and checked in for the night. Daddy described his standard honeymoon package to his brother-in-law.

"The way we work it, Shorty stays in the car while I register for the room. Then, once we're settled in, Shorty gets the ice while I set the thermostat to working. While she fixes our glasses and tunes in the right channel on the TV, I open the Vienna sausages and pop the top on a fresh 2-liter bottle of the Real Thing. A Coca-Cola never tastes so good as when you're propped up on a motel bed with clean sheets underneath you and a box of Ritz crackers nearby.

"When we get ready for some real food, we order up a plate of fried chicken delivered right to the room. Women love room service. If my baby doll wants a pot of coffee, I order that too — even if there's a coffeemaker in the room. Women set a high value on having a pot of coffee come to the room. It's like a diamond ring to them. Don't even ask questions about it. In the long run, Tommy, it's the best two dollars and a half you will ever spend on a honeymoon."

It seemed like a good time to join them, so I did.

"Come give me a little sugar, honey," Uncle Tommy said when he saw me standing in the kitchen doorway.

He was sitting at the oak table with a cup of hot coffee steaming in front of him. I stepped into the circle of his familiar embrace and kissed the top of his head. He used to smell like machine oil, but he didn't anymore. Not since he retired. Now he wore one of those expensive men's colognes. I didn't recognize it — a gift from Bonnie, probably. "How's my beautiful girl?" he asked.

I stopped myself from saying "Patty Kate is fine" because everyone knew that my younger sister was the pretty one. "Everything's great."

"Even after this old man gave you a scare?" Uncle Tommy asked.

He watched my face, his eyes searching mine for the truth. He was the big brother in my mother's family, and he looked the part. He was built like John Wayne.

"He did give me a scare," I replied. "But the doctor said if you are going to have heart trouble, arrhythmia is the best kind to have. They can control it."

"I have had heart trouble ever since I met your mother and she took me to the gravel pit," Daddy said, pressing his hand to his chest. Underneath the white T-shirt he wore were fading burn marks from the electric paddles the doctors had used.

"I did not take you to a lover's lane before we were married," Mother corrected him.

"Did you or did you not take me to the gravel pit?" Daddy asked.

"It was a mistake. I've told you that a hundred times. I asked some-one at the Montgomery Fair for directions to the drive-in."

"As if that's any better than the gravel pit," Daddy interjected.

"I like movies. There's nothing wrong with that," Mother sniffed. "You like them too, Mr. Bond . . . James Bond."

"But we didn't go to the drive-in. We went to the gravel pit," Daddy reminded her.

"But we didn't stay," she replied tartly.

Daddy rubbed his hands together gleefully. "Shorty, I knew you were going to be a handful when you threw that Wrigley spearmint gum wrapper down on my clean floor." Daddy turned to me and began to tell the story I could recite from memory about how he and Mother met. "I was sweeping the hallway at The Fair when your Mother walked by in a red sweater and a long black skirt. She was wearing some high-heeled black patent leather shoes that showed off her legs. She was the prettiest thing I'd ever seen."

Mother sat down on the oak bench opposite me. "I wouldn't date your daddy for a long time. I thought he might be a drinker because his eyes were always bloodshot. But I found out he was pulling a dou-ble shift for another man who was sick. Once I knew that, I dated him," Mother explained one more time.

"And that was all she wrote. Not three weeks later she was taking me to the gravel pit," Daddy teased.

"To the Justice of the Peace," Mother amended, her brown eyes gleaming. Their wedding picture was kept in the family album but not on display. In her haste to marry Daddy, Mother had bought a wedding dress just a day before the ceremony, and all these years later, she was still dismayed that in the picture — if you looked hard enough — you could tell that her underslip was too short for the tea-length dress. *Girls, don't stand in a lit doorway in a dress without a slip.* Mother knew the rules, but she had broken one accidentally on her wedding day. The memory had haunted her ever since.

"That's what Bonnie and I are going to do," Uncle Tommy said, leaning forward to cut himself another piece of pound cake. When he was finished, I took the knife and cut myself a slice. I held it in my hand like a sandwich.

"Are you going to bring Bonnie over soon?" Mother asked, pushing a napkin in my direction to catch the cake crumbs. She was wearing her cut-off jeans and a University of Alabama T-shirt that matched the one she had sent her younger brother Joe-Joe out in Arizona. He was an Alabama football fan, and she wore it on the days she was lonely for him.

"Bonnie's at work today," Uncle Tommy said. He was proud of his stylish bride-to-be, who was a fashion consultant at Gayfers, which had bought out the Montgomery Fair. Bonnie worked in Finer Fashions, where the clothes were the most expensive. "I'll bring her soon. I've told her that you are the writer in the family," he said, turning to me. "By the way, I heard you got paid for a story this time, Daffodil," he said with pride.

I nodded. I had always written stories, but only in the last year or so had I been submitting them to magazines and newspapers. A few places had published my stories and paid me in contributor's copies. But now they were sending me checks.

"I want a copy of it. Are you ever going to put me in one of your stories?"

"Maybe I already have, and you just don't know it," I teased, as

Mother went to her kitchen desk to retrieve a Xerox copy of the newest piece I'd written about Daddy and her.

"Your mother would tell me if I were in one of the stories," Uncle Tommy asserted.

"Maybe she doesn't know. Maybe I have a few secrets," I said.

They all looked at me to see if I was the kind of person who could keep secrets. Then they grinned. They knew me too well.

Mother handed the copy to Uncle Tommy. "Thank you, honey. I'll show it to Bonnie." His big bear-paw of a hand easily engulfed the story entitled "Dad Goes Bananas," and I wished in that moment that it was a better story.

"So many words," he mused admiringly as he folded it. "How do you sell these stories?"

"Put them in an envelope and mail them off," I replied.

"She steals my stamps," Daddy pretended to complain.

Uncle Tommy's eyes grinned at me, and he winked. "If you need more stamps, you call me. I'll bring you some."

And he would have. When we were growing up and Daddy was working the midnight shift at the air force base, he slept during the day. Mother didn't drive, so if we needed anything, we called Uncle Tommy. One hot summer day my mother told me to call him up and tell him we were out of Coca-Colas. As if it were an emergency, Uncle Tommy came later that afternoon with a whole case of twenty-four little bottles — the best kind. They cost $2.40 for the case, but he wouldn't take any money for them.

"I can drive to the post office," I said.

"Doesn't matter how old you get. You know you can call me if you need me," Uncle Tommy said, his gaze holding mine. He wasn't talking about stamps. He rose and walked to the front door, then turned. He filled the space, and the size of him was comforting. "You two gonna stand up with me?"

A new gold chain sparkled at his throat, an unlikely fashion choice for a former machinist. Bonnie had brought some sparkle into my uncle's life in more ways than one.

"You're really ready to tie the knot?" Daddy asked. He walked over to the door, and Mother followed him.

"We're going to elope, and when we go, we want you two with us. You too, Daffodil, if you're not too busy writing your stories."

I grinned neutrally. I wouldn't go. My parents, the experts on love, would. I didn't fit into that group.

"I don't think you'll go wrong taking Bonnie to the Shoney Inn. Shorty always likes it," Daddy interrupted before I needed to answer.

"Boys," Mother piped up, "a woman who works in fine fashions might want to stay in some other kind of motel — or even a fine hotel — on her honeymoon."

Uncle Tommy laughed out loud. "It's Bonnie, Lola. Bonnie." And in that moment Uncle Tommy traveled through time on Bonnie's name. One more time, incredibly, although he was standing in our doorway, he was also the seventeen-year-old boy who was going steady with his high-school sweetheart. He was that Tommy. The boy who had broken his arm at school and gone by the doctor's office alone to get it set so it wouldn't worry his Ma later. He could just tell his Ma, Yes, it was broken, but it's set now, and everything is all right. He was the big brother who had campaigned for his younger sister to be voted Most Beautiful at Autauga County High and had succeeded as the champion of my mother's beauty. He was that Tommy — the boy Bonnie had loved when she was seventeen too.

With that one name and in that moment, Mother saw immediately, just as I did, that Bonnie would relish the Shoney Inn and room service with fried chicken and hot coffee coming to the room and only costing two dollars and a half a pot, because even after forty years had passed, he was still Tommy, and when she was with him, she was his girl — she was Bonnie.

We all lingered at the door as our Tommy slowly drove off toward his future. As always, he waved out the window as he left us. We waved back in sweet unison, our hearts beating in rhythm again to the tempo of true love, because he who had been love for so long to so many people had found love again.

From the Family Album . . .

Dad Goes Bananas

"Can you help me out by eating a banana?"

"No, sir, I cannot," I replied evenly. Daddy frequently tries to ply me with food. Sometimes I brace myself to go into a room where he is snacking with a "no" on my lips.

"We're on the verge of losing two of them. Hate to see 'em go to waste."

I looked at the bananas he thought were in danger of expiring. I had seen worse-looking bananas on the grocery store shelf.

"Why don't you eat one?" I suggested.

It was the question he had been waiting to hear.

Dad plucked one of the two bananas, peeled it, and took his first bite.

"You know what this is, don't you?" he asked.

Recognizing a rhetorical question when I heard one, I did not answer.

"This is pure potassium. Good for you. No sugar. No caffeine. A banana is the perfect food."

"And cheap," I said.

"That too," he agreed, nodding approvingly. "Not like that stuff your mother usually brings into the house to try and kill me. Costs like the devil and is loaded with chemicals and fat."

"Mother's not trying to kill you," I said. "She cooks to please you."

He ignored my argument, offering one of his own. "What do you think all that ice cream is doing in the freezer?"

Mother returned from the kitchen, where she had been putting on a fresh pot of coffee. I heard the familiar gurgle of the water beginning to perk. "Why do you think the ice cream is just for you?" she asked. "There are other people living here in this house who might like to have some of that ice cream if you would give them half a chance at it."

"Can't let ice cream stay in the freezer that long, taking up space," Dad interrupted. "It costs money to keep food frozen."

Mother looked at me and mouthed the words, "Your daddy is a glutton."

Dad doesn't look like a piggish eater. At six feet and 170 pounds, my daddy is a good-looking guy who has always had a nice physique. His appetite is healthy, and since a problem with his heart has been diagnosed, he is health-conscious. What that means is that he talks about what he should and should not eat, and then he holds Mother responsible for his decisions.

"You know," he said, "I had to cut down on caffeine on account of my heart, and your mother still makes the hardcore stuff all the time. She knows the smell of coffee perking is irresistible to a dying man. Do you hear that coffeepot perking again? I'm telling you, I think the woman is trying to kill me."

"If I were trying to kill you, you'd be dead," Mother replied succinctly. "I've got some instant decaf in the kitchen, and it's been there for some time! I'll make you some whenever you say you want it."

"I'd like a cup of coffee right now," Dad said, chewing assiduously. "Go good with this banana."

"I'll make you a cup of the decaf, and I'll drink a cup of the perked," Mother said archly.

"I hate to put you to the trouble of boiling water. Why don't I just share your cup of coffee? A half a cup won't hurt the old ticker."

"While I'm on my feet, do you want me to hand you that other banana?" she asked on her way back to the kitchen.

"Haven't got this one down good yet," he replied seriously.

"Looks like you might be able to finish it," she observed dryly.

When Mother returned, she brought the second banana and a mug of steaming coffee — the hardcore stuff — with sugar in it. When Daddy discovered the coffee was sweet, he slurped down the whole cup, forgetting he had volunteered to share, and then he turned his attention back to the perfect fruit.

Over the top of the second banana, he said, "Did you see how your mother tempted me with that cup of caffeine? Caffeine is an irritant. Could throw my heart out of whack. And now she's stuffing this other banana down me. I'm not sure just how much potassium a body can tolerate. And I've still got those ice-cream sandwiches in the freezer that I need to eat."

Mother stood in the doorway that led to the kitchen with her empty coffee cup. "I think I'll have an ice-cream sandwich," she announced. She looked at me, and I nodded yes.

Daddy looked concerned. "Ice cream is loaded with fat. Those can't be good for you. I could just share half of yours," he suggested to me, taking large bites of the second banana.

Mother returned with three ice-cream treats. Daddy hurriedly finished the second banana and began to peel the paper off the ice-cream sandwich. He eyed Mother's refilled coffee cup, interested.

She reached over and drew the steaming cup toward herself.

Daddy frowned, taking a bite. "I tell you, all this food your mother brings into the house would kill an ordinary man."

Neither one of us argued with him, because we believed him.

3

The Midas Touch

"What do you hear?" Daddy asked, handing me the stethoscope.

It was Friday night, and he was sitting on the end of the long green sofa in the living room. He should have been getting dressed for our family-night supper. I stopped on my way to the kitchen, pressed the round diaphragm of the stethoscope against his chest, and listened. "Ka-thump. Ka-thump. Ka-thump," I said.

He peered up at me from an angle, his blind green eye clouded now. His blue one was clear and, like him in so many ways, still innocent. "Does it sound like it's in rhythm?" he asked.

I listened another minute. "Your heartbeat sounds normal to me."

"If you say my heart is in rhythm, I guess I'm okay."

"I think you are probably just excited about the real-estate deal," I said.

Daddy had finally bought a parcel of land in Autauga County and borrowed fifty thousand dollars to pay for it. Daddy's fourteen-word jewel of an ad to sell the land had run in the morning newspaper, and the phone had been ringing all day. He was excited by the response, and that excitement made him listen to his heart in between the telephone conversations. He had been giving out driving instructions to callers.

"Why don't you get dressed?" I encouraged. "The girls will be here soon. Tommy and Bonnie too, maybe. What time is your first appointment tomorrow?" I asked, as he moved to the bathroom sink to shave.

I leaned against the door frame to keep him company. I always had, ever since he had worked the midnight shift at the air force base. It was when we talked — he on his way to work, I on my way to bed.

"The first appointment is for 9:30. I would have said 8:30, but your mother isn't a morning person."

"Does Mother know she's going?"

He looked at me quizzically in the mirror. "Why wouldn't she know she's going?" He looked left, then right, checking his sideburns.

"You're even," I said, as our eyes met in the mirror. Daddy finished his shaving ritual and slapped on some Old Spice cologne. I inhaled deeply, loving the familiar scent.

"'Cause she's going to be up late tonight if Bonnie and Tommy come by," I said, shrugging. "You should tell her."

"Tell me what?" Mother asked. "Will you watch the dinner while I comb out my hair?" It was still in rollers. Little yellow and pink plastic ones. Mother figured that if she didn't let her hair down until the last minute and sprayed it real well, the curls would keep through Sunday.

I went to the kitchen to stir the simmering pots of country-fried steak, shoe-peg corn, and turnip greens while Daddy explained that they had an appointment in the morning.

"Nine-thirty in the morning! Are you crazy?" Mother exclaimed.

"Don't get all riled up. I'll wake you up in plenty of time."

"You live to wake me up," Mother said, exasperated. "You cannot stand for me to be asleep. I cannot even take a nap in the afternoon without you coming over and saying, 'Lola, Lola, do you want to get up?' I don't know why it bothers you for people to sleep."

"It doesn't bother me except when there's work to be done," Daddy explained.

"Some work gets done at night. You just like the work done in the morning."

"Settle down now, Shorty. Let's not worry about it tonight. Every day has sufficient trouble unto itself."

Mother switched gears on him before he got to preaching. Daddy still occasionally filled in for the regular preacher at church, and he often inserted mini-sermons into his conversations. He couldn't help it.

"Did you get the person's phone number?" she asked. "You could change that appointment to later in the day."

"It'd be too hot by then," Daddy said, dismissing the idea. "Besides, you know how I feel about putting off chores. I don't like to do it. I can always go by myself. Let's not worry about it. I didn't mean to upset the apple cart."

"You get on out of here and let me comb out my hair. You know you don't like hairspray."

"Don't be mad at me."

"I'm not mad. I'm just trying to finish getting dressed. You've known all week long that we were having company tonight."

"It's not company. It's just our regular Friday-night supper, and it's just our family."

The phone rang again. "I'll get it," I called out, snagging the receiver. "It's for you, Daddy. It's about the land."

Daddy hurried to the phone, clearing his voice the way he did before he led the prayer at church. "It's about a forty-five-minute commute to Montgomery," he said as he launched into the directions. Then, lowering his voice, he said, "I'll be there in the morning showing it to another caller, but you're welcome to come out and look around. I'll be there until noon."

He hung up the phone, his eyes catching mine. I shook my head. "Your mother's not really mad. Besides, I think most people want a little piece of land, don't you?" he asked nervously.

A need to respond was cut short by the front door opening. Julie Ann arrived with her husband, Big Jody, and their two-year-old son. Julie Ann placed a basket of fresh tomatoes on the kitchen counter. Her complexion was rosy, her long auburn hair shiny. She was pregnant and it agreed with her. "Big Jody thought you'd like these," she said. My brother-in-law managed a grocery store, and he often brought us fresh produce.

"Anything to eat?" Big Jody asked, dismissing the possibility of gratitude being expressed.

"No, we don't have anything to eat!" I replied tartly.

"It smells like you're not telling me the truth. Don't tell me that's country-fried steak."

"Okay," I said, leaning against the sink.

"And turnip greens?" he asked, peeking under a pan lid. Big Jody smiled. It was his signature smile — open and honest, like him.

"Yes. The greens are from Mr. Simpson's turnip patch next door."

He raised an eyebrow.

"We didn't steal them. He gives them to us."

"I believe you," he said. "What about the fruit salad with those little oranges in it?"

"Chilling in the refrigerator."

Big Jody tested the hot oven. "Don't tell me I can feel cornbread baking."

I sighed deeply. "Only yeast rolls."

He shook his head, disappointed. I didn't blame him. Mother's cornbread was special, and the absence of it deserved to be grieved.

The coffeepot began to drip, and the sound startled him. Big Jody didn't drink coffee. It was his only flaw. "Mother made plenty of sweet tea," I told him.

"Your mother always puts enough sugar in her tea."

I nodded while I poured a glass for him. "There's also fudge and her Coca-Cola Jello." Big Jody took a swig of tea. "Do you suppose your mother would make some cornbread after the rolls are done?"

"She might. You could ask her. She loves you."

"I know," Big Jody said. "Most women do."

"That'll be our little secret," I replied as Mary Ellen arrived. Her husband Steve, a high-school football coach, was out of town at a game, but their three children were with her. Lola Leigh and Little Jerry promptly gravitated to the television in the living room, and Mary Ellen settled Matthew, her youngest, onto his granddaddy's lap.

"Do you need me to do something?" she asked, placing a fresh loaf of banana bread on the counter.

"You could take out the rolls and turn up the oven to 425°," I said.

I poured a little oil into the cast-iron skillet and placed it in the oven to heat.

Mother came in while Mary Ellen was pouring the cornmeal into a bowl. I added the milk.

"How does my hair look?" Mother asked, automatically cracking the egg into the soupy mixture. "Your Daddy was talking to me through the door, and I got in a hurry. He knows I don't like to be talked to while I'm in the bathroom."

"He's got that land on his mind, and your hair looks beautiful," I assured her. Her soft brown curls were shiny and well-sprayed.

"Is the pan ready?" she asked. I opened the oven door and flicked a drop of water into the skillet. The sizzle meant it was hot enough. Using a mitt, I retrieved the pan, resting it on the stove while Mother poured the batter.

Big Jody returned for a refill. "You pay attention and learn to cook like your mama, and you'll get a man yet."

"I'm learning as fast as I can," I said. It was our standing joke.

Mother started making plates then, serving from the stove, and my sisters and I became the assembly line that passed along the steaming food. We sat down as our own plates were made. The skillet of hot cornbread appeared last, cut into a dozen pie-shaped wedges and slathered with real butter. I sat down right before Mother, and one more time we were all squeezed around the oak table. Only Patty Kate was missing. She was running late.

"Shorty, you've outdone yourself," Daddy said, his mouth full of turnip greens. "Those tomatoes are good too, Julie. And I'm saving that banana bread until I don't have to share it, Mary Ellen." His smile was mischievous.

"I'll make you another loaf anytime you want it," Mary Ellen promised.

And she would. Mary Ellen baked fruit breads. I made lemon meringue pie. Patty Kate baked coconut cream pies, and Julie Ann had perfected a peanut-butter spice cake — a recipe she had learned from her mother-in-law, a woman she still called Mrs. Helms.

We all liked to cook, and we all cooked for Daddy — anything he wanted, anytime he wanted it. He liked to eat, and we loved him. Cooking was just another way to express that.

Daddy finished his meal first — a fast eater, and faster yet because the phone continued to ring through the dinner hour, hurrying him.

"Let it ring," Mother urged, her brow furrowing at the interruptions.

But Daddy couldn't. The last time he came back to the table, he announced, "Tommy and Bonnie aren't coming. They are . . . detained." He winked at Mother.

"There's always tomorrow," she said briskly, ignoring the wink. "They've got a lot to do."

"I'll say," Daddy agreed as the phone rang again. He kept answering it and telling people where the land was and that he would be there in the morning, and Mother averted her gaze because she wasn't adjusted yet to the idea of having to get up that early.

But she would. She had been protesting early risings for years, but she always got up when Daddy wanted her to.

After the dessert, the dominoes came out, and people rotated at the oak table to take a turn at the domino boneyard, and in between, when players were studying their pieces and someone started to hum, the singing began. We were a family of singers, breaking into song like they did in musicals.

Patty Kate arrived just as we began Daddy's favorite, "Love Lifted Me."

During the song, Patty Kate made herself a plate and then perched on the corner of the oak bench where she always sat. Her thin frame still fit easily into what had become close quarters for the rest of us.

When we finished the refrain, Mother asked her, "How was your week?"

Before she could answer, Daddy asked, "Did you learn anything at that university?"

Patty Kate was studying psychology at the University of Alabama, and she had discovered Freud and Jung and the theory that dreams could tell the truth about our interior lives. When we tried to get her to interpret a couple of our dreams, she declined: "I can't do that. They're your dreams. Only you can interpret what they mean."

The mention of dreams reminded us of the late hour, and as if on cue, sleepy children began to whimper to go home. Mother handed Mary Ellen a plate of food she had fixed for Steve, and Mary Ellen promised he would eat it. Big Jody handed her a tomato to take home with it.

Patty Kate and I cleaned up the kitchen, moving in a rhythm learned through years of sharing work. But there really wasn't much to do. Mother always cleaned up as she cooked, and we had been taught to do the same.

After she made the coffeepot for the next morning, Patty Kate disappeared into her bedroom, and I went to mine. I flopped onto my bed and resumed reading a mystery by John D. McDonald. He was so good at describing people's eyes that you could look right into their souls.

Patty Kate's bed creaked, and the next thing I knew she was talking low on the phone to someone. I tried not to listen, but it was hard. She talked a long time, and then her light went out while I was still making notes in my journal for some stories I wanted to write. I don't know what time I fell over into sleep, but I woke up to the smell of coffee perking.

I heard the familiar thump of the morning newspaper landing at the front door, and I knew that Daddy would open that paper immediately and check to see if his fourteen-word ad was in there the second day, just like he had paid for it to be.

After he drank his coffee and read his Bible and said his prayers, he took Mother a cup and placed it by her hand, and said, "Lola, Lola, do you want to get up?"

"No," she said, like she always did. But she got up anyway.

And then she resisted the call of the crossword puzzle and the Jumble and combed her hair gingerly, spraying it some more, praying that it would last through Sunday, and she and Daddy drove off toward the land and the strangers who had called about it.

The phone continued to ring off the wall, and I took down names and numbers like I'd been taught. Patty Kate came out of her room very dressed up, grabbed her car keys, and said in a hurry, "I'm going to the mall." She didn't ask me to go with her. I wrote that down about her in my journal after she left.

When I heard the Cadillac return, I peeped out the window. Mother and Daddy were walking up to the house hand in hand.

"You've had a lot of phone calls," I announced, waving the sheet of notepaper.

"I'll call them back later," Daddy said.

"Are you all right?" I asked. I often asked that question.

"Your Daddy's feeling pretty good," Mother reassured me.

"Did you sell one?" I asked, grinning hopefully.

"Yes," he said, pausing for the news to sink in. "And then I sold another one and another one."

"Your Daddy sold every one of those lots!" Mother said, her eyes shining. "Sold them all in one morning. Just him and his old orange briefcase."

I wondered if the excitement would make Daddy want to pull out his stethoscope and listen to his heart, but he was too busy being happy to be worried about his health.

"Cars were lined up all the way out the dirt road to the street," he said jubilantly. He turned to Mother, and she smiled with a joy that was deep and mysterious and expectant.

"Your daddy named a road after me," she announced, shaking her head in wonder. Her sprayed curls bounced resiliently. "When we made that last right turn, there was a sign that read 'Lola Lane.' He named that road after me. It's official."

"It will be on the city map and everything," Daddy said proudly. "'Lola Lane' is better than 'Lola Drive,' isn't it?" he asked me suddenly.

I nodded. "Much."

"Your daddy . . . ," Mother said, as she went to the kitchen to put on a pot of coffee, ". . . is full of surprises. Lola Lane." She repeated the words with obvious pleasure.

I looked at Daddy then. His shoulders were back, and his eyes were bright with satisfaction. He said with wonder, surprised by his own Midas touch, "I told you girls that most people want a little piece of land."

From the Family Album . . .

The Midnight Shift

The house settles down the same way every night. Finally, Mother tells her mother good night on the telephone. The same boards creak as she checks the locks on the doors that Daddy has already checked. She makes a glass of ice water to take to the room where Daddy is lightly sleeping. He rouses when she comes to bed and says, "Is that you?"

"No, it's not me. It's someone else," she replies.

"Okay," he says, "but don't wake the girls."

There are no other girls home full-time. There is usually only me now.

I am the girl who hears the conversations and the other sounds in the house at night, for since Daddy retired, I am the one who keeps the midnight shift.

I read. I listen. I stare out the window at the moon. "The moon is a harsh mistress," my oldest sister sings. When I see starlight, I can hear Mary Ellen's voice. That's how her voice sounds: like starlight. Not like Julie Ann's, whose voice is like a waterfall. Patty Kate's voice is solitary but hopeful, and in that way, though not as loud, somehow stronger than either one. Voices are harder to describe than eyes, I think.

I make more notes about other images and sounds that might fit into stories I want to write. I hold onto my memories this way while I plan ahead, marveling that just recently I really did go to England to the William Wordsworth Summer Conference. Wordsworth's great-nephews ran it. Everyone drank tea and talked about poetry with the respect it deserved. No one dared to call Wordsworth only a nature poet. Iris Murdoch was the keynote speaker.

She and her husband sat down at my table for a big English break-fast just like they eat in the movies. There, over eggs and a rasher of bacon, Iris Murdoch asked if I was a writer too, and I said, "Not really," and she asked me again with a sharp glint in her otherwise-shy gaze, and I said, "I am sort of writing a book."

"What's it about?" she asked.

"The experience of time," I replied.

"Fascinating," she said.

Fascinating.

I hadn't been able to write a whole story since. Just fragments. Writer's block? I didn't know, as I had never run into wordlessness before.

Something taps against my window — a branch from the nearby tree, probably. In that sound, however, I travel backward even further in time to when Daddy was still working the midnight shift at the local air-force base, where he was a troubleshooter for anything that broke during the long night. On his way to work, Daddy knocked gently on my window to say good night. I always waited for the sound of his fingertips tapping on the glass. His hand. My father's hand. A preacher's hand. A working man's hand. The same hand that had taught me how to hold a hammer, use a screwdriver, wrap the pipes in winter. A hand with a Midas touch.

I pick up my pen and clipboard and begin to write this story from a childhood memory:

My Father's Hand

I kneel outside the room where Daddy teaches Sunday school, although he tells me each week before we go off to our separate classes not to do it.

I cannot help it. I try not to. But my teacher, Mrs. Echols, lets my class out exactly when the bell rings, and as I walk past Daddy's classroom, I hear his voice and I freeze outside his door.

I'll just take a peek, I think. I drop to my knees and peer through the keyhole.

See his hand. The hand that held the pliers, the level, the wooden measuring rule that folds out, *flip-flip, flip-flop.*

My head hits the doorknob and rattles it. I wince. People go past me, but no one asks me what I am doing. I should go upstairs to the sanctuary. Mother is waiting for us on the pew where my family always sits.

But he is talking, and although I cannot hear what he is saying, I cannot leave the sound of his voice.

Daddy? Daddy?

That's my daddy in there that people listen to. He's the man who talks about Jesus. Do you know who Jesus is?

Yes, Daddy.

And then he got us baptized, one by one, as soon as we could hold his gaze and answer firmly, "Jesus is the Son of God. He is the only doorway to God the Father."

Kneeling in the doorway that leads to my father's hand, his rich preacher's voice, I believe in Jesus' gift of himself. I have a Daddy who keeps giving himself away in good works. It made perfect sense to me that the Son of God would do this too. I sigh in appreciation, in a joy that can't be quenched, in an eagerness for him to make the final prayer and say "Amen" and open the door and let the people out so that I can just be waiting here for him, kind of like I just happened to be passing by.

Except the door opens all of a sudden, and one more time I am eye-to-eye with the adults who are still sitting in their Sunday school chairs. They bite their lips, trying not to smile.

"What are you doing here again?" Daddy asks, exasperated. "I've told you where to go when your class lets out." He takes a deep breath, shakes his head. "Come on in."

I stand up and walk over to his side and bury my face against his leg. His hand finds mine. He speaks, quoting words from the Bible — such beautiful poetry! — and then says, "Shall we pray?"

I watch the faces of the people while he prays. Some of

them don't close their eyes. They wink at me, and I let my eyes smile, but I don't let my mouth do it in case my daddy is watching. I won't look up. He might be really mad at me. He could be. He has told me not to wait for him here because he sometimes runs late. The Spirit of the Living Lord doesn't punch a clock.

He gives me all kinds of advice, and then he gives me orders.

Go to the bathroom.

Find one of your sisters.

Get a drink of water.

I can't do any of it. Because I heard the sound of his voice, and when I looked through the keyhole, I saw his hand go by. My father's hand. It was just on the other side of the door, and I couldn't not wait for it — couldn't not reach for it.

Even his displeasure was not too high a price to pay for the waiting.

When the class is dismissed, people shake my father's hand — the other one. He shakes hands backwards, explaining that his daughter won't let go of his right hand.

I grin up at people who offer me pieces of gum, which I do not accept. That would be going too far.

They pat me on the head. "Don't be too hard on her, Jerry."

He waves aside their advice, but when they're gone, he asks, "Why do you do that? Every week I ask you not to, and every week you interrupt my class so that I have to open the door and let you in. What do you have to say for yourself?"

I shrug. I do not have the words to explain, to tell him that I heard his voice, heard him talking about light and dark and love and Jesus, saw his hand, and I could not leave.

"This is Sunday school, and it's where we learn about the love of God. We have to take that very seriously," he says, "because it's very serious."

"Yes, sir," I say.

"We have to love the Father with all our hearts, minds, souls, and wills. That's why we are here."

I nod as we make the awkward walk up the narrow wooden staircase to the sanctuary. It is the room reserved for worship, but it was downstairs on my knees beside my daddy's door where I first knew the love that drew me and would not let me go.

II

FAMILY LAND

4

The Dream House

"The next time you come out, bring a pair of pajamas with you and plan on spending the night," Daddy said to Uncle Tommy, who had driven the twenty miles from his home to Mother and Daddy's new dream house. It had five bedrooms and four bathrooms, and there was plenty of land. There were separate lots assigned to each of us daughters, so that we could build our own houses on the property. Daddy called it the family commune.

Daddy and Mother had been the first ones to move three years earlier, leaving me behind at my job in Montgomery. About a year later, Mary Ellen and Steve accepted the farthest lot at the end of the acreage. Lonely for my family, I took the lot beside them. It was a woodsy piece of property with a creek that ran behind it and a white, sandy beach. There were two more lots reserved for Patty Kate and Julie Ann, who were, incomprehensibly, living separate lives in other states.

"I'll cook you up a pot of pinto beans and cornbread next time. Won't be too long before tomatoes will make," Mother promised her brother Tommy.

Spying me, Uncle Tommy called out, "Did you walk over here to see me, honey?" He eyed my cartload of sticks suspiciously.

"You know I did," I said. "You aren't gonna spend the night?"

"No. Just dropped in for a cup of coffee. Your mama wants to feed a man to death."

43

"She'll do it," I agreed.

That was one of the reasons I was out in the woods picking up sticks. I wanted to take off some of the weight Mama's cooking had put on. Instead of forty-five minutes of *Jazzercise*, I had assigned myself the calorie-burning task of picking up broken tree limbs in the woods. I liked it.

"It's a shame you have to rush off, Tommy," Daddy interrupted.

"Been here all afternoon. I don't call that rushing off," Uncle Tommy said. "Just came out to get rid of some motor oil. We've been burning tree stumps," he explained. "Looks like you're gonna need to do some burning too."

"When I get the time," I agreed.

"Never enough of that," he said.

"Don't I know it? Just the other day, Mary Ellen and I were sitting out in her swing saying how much we missed long summer days. Summer used to be a lot longer than it is now." I loved living next door to my sister again. We drank coffee together, traded good books, and swapped dreams.

"Sunday afternoons were the longest days of the week," Uncle Tommy said.

"That's because preachers used to be more long-winded than they are now."

"Yeah. Even the preachers have learned how to tell time," he said.

We all hesitated while considering whether that was more good than bad. Though sermons had become repetitious to me in theme and content, the rhythm of a preacher's voice could be very relaxing.

"Now, Sundays are just like any other day. Did you pick up all those limbs by yourself?" Uncle Tommy asked, changing the subject.

I expect that he thought we might get into a talk about religion, but I wasn't going to. Instead, we surveyed the three separate stacks of fallen tree branches and sticks I had gathered.

Daddy spoke up. "I don't know what's got into her, Tommy. I saw her out there the other day shoveling red clay to fill in the potholes in the road."

"Baby, that's something men are supposed to do," Uncle Tommy said.

"Yes, sir. I know that. And if I could find one to do it better than I do and as cheaply, I'd turn the road work over to him."

They all nodded approvingly. I hadn't lost my mind yet. I smiled my good-niece, sensible-daughter smile and began to unload my cart. I was starting a new burn pile. I figured they were all impressed, but no one said so.

"I've got some fresh coffee inside," Mother offered.

"Wouldn't mind a cup of coffee," I replied.

Their relief was almost tangible. They don't really believe that women should sweat.

"I'm going on, then," Uncle Tommy said.

He hugged me good-bye, holding my face against his chest, where for a moment I was a little girl again. He smelled of machine oil like he used to, and the outdoors — like home.

When he was in his car, he said through the window, his eyes smiling, "Good to see ya."

"See ya again," we promised in a chorus. We had said the words all of our lives, but every time it was hard to let him go.

We watched silently as he drove away.

"Don't you snap off your fingernails doing that kind of work?" Mother asked, suddenly irritable, ostensibly with me, but it was really because her brother had left, and no matter how long he stays, Uncle Tommy always leaves too soon.

"Yes, ma'am. Broke them all off right down to the quick. Can't have fingernails and do any real work."

"How much longer you figure on keeping these woods picked up?" Daddy asked.

"Well, I've lost nineteen pounds on this afternoon-workout plan of mine, and I want to get rid of another eleven. At five pounds a month, that'll make it right at two more months. The rest of the summer."

"That's all right, then. As long as you've got a good reason to be out in that sun," Mother said.

"Yes, ma'am. Dad, can I have another cartload of your fill dirt for the potholes?"

"You know you can have anything I've got. But you're not ever going to get those potholes filled."

"Maybe not," I agreed.

"You're gonna lose that other eleven pounds. I know that. Not that you need to. You can think what you want, but to me, you're the perfect size." He smiled at me, and I could not resist the power of his love.

When we went inside the dream house, I stopped and took a long look at myself in the pink-tinted mirror Dad hung by the front door after the house was first built. "That's so my girls can always see themselves in the pink of health," Daddy had said. I brushed aside my damp bangs and grinned. I was pink and healthy.

I joined my parents at the same old oak table in the huge kitchen that ran the entire length of the house. The senior portraits of my sisters and me were now hung over a fireplace that was for looks only. Daddy didn't like the idea of a real fire burning where his loved ones were, and that fear included the pictures of his loved ones. The mantel clock still made its snuffling commentary on the hour.

Upstairs our old bedroom suites were in rooms that had been assigned to us, even though none of us lived there. That fact didn't affect the truth. "This is your real home," Daddy said of the dream house.

He and Mother had told us that from the minute Daddy finally decided to build it.

After all the years in their old house, Mother was reluctant to make the move. She belonged to a club we didn't usually mention: she didn't drive. She didn't want to leave Montgomery, a big city that had taxis, and move to Millbrook, where there was no public transportation.

But Daddy was persistent. He reminded Mother that she had initially said no to the idea of air conditioning, and didn't she love air conditioning? And she hadn't liked the idea of television either, and now didn't she love television? And there would be plenty of land to subdivide so that each daughter could have her own house and land if she wanted it, and wouldn't Mother love to live next door to her girls again?

Mother had looked up from her crossword puzzle and asked, "What kind of house exactly?"

Then Daddy pulled out the plans for the dream house and took Mother on a fingertip tour of the floor plan. "This shows an attached garage, but we'll enclose it and make it like a small apartment where all your grandchildren can play. It'll have a private bath, and we'll put a really big TV in there," he promised. "And here's the den that leads to the kitchen that runs the length of the house. I'll give you a wall full of windows so that you can look out on the back yard. And at night, the moon will sit right outside. I'll arrange it."

The promise of moonlight had done its part to woo Mother across the river, and now we were sitting right beside those windows. Mother placed a cup of coffee in front of me. "How about a good old heaping spoonful of sugar?" she asked. She knew I was dieting, but she loved sugar in her own coffee.

"I could use the energy," I replied honestly.

Happily, Mother added the sugar, and in my acceptance I was forgiven the abuse of my fingernails. The irritation she felt over Uncle Tommy leaving dissolved as she stirred my coffee.

"You've done some good work out there," Daddy said.

"Makes my muscles feel good. Seems more respectable, too, than hopping around in a leotard and tights."

"I don't know why anyone would wear those outfits," Daddy agreed. "Just a money-making scheme some advertising company came up with. Never seen a woman yet who looks that good in one of those exercise getups."

How silly I looked in tights and a leotard wasn't the reason I'd gone into the woods day after day. I let go of counting minutes when I was picking up sticks. What I wanted from summer was a sense of timelessness. I had found it here and there. In the woods — in broken tree limbs, in the secret places where huckleberries hide and ripen, in the unmistakable and not unpleasant dark odors of aged, winter leaves metamorphosing into soil. In my parents, who always had the time to be hospitable. In Mary Ellen, who checked on the grapevines in her yard with leisurely pleasure.

"So, what have you two been doing?" I asked my folks, downing the sweet coffee. I asked them this question every day.

"We stay pretty busy," Daddy said. "You get any good writing done?"

"Don't know yet," I answered. "Maybe. Maybe not."

He was accustomed to this peculiar response. I said it often now, since I had quit my job with the newspaper and wrote full-time in my little house in the woods.

"Have you seen your sister?" Mother asked, and just as she spoke, sunlight poured in through the panel of kitchen windows. My parents glowed in it. It fell upon their lovely, familiar hands, casting their larger-than-life shadows on the wall.

"Not since yesterday. Probably see her in a few minutes. She likes to take a turn around her yard. Her grapes look good this year, and she has the biggest blueberry bush I've ever seen."

"You want to spend the night?" Mother asked suddenly.

I laughed softly. "I live right next door. Why would I spend the night?"

"You just might want to," she said.

"Not tonight. I'm reading a good book by Robert B. Parker. A Spenser novel. I've just discovered Spenser, and I want to read the whole series before the next one comes out." I put my cup in the sink and ran water in it like I'd been taught.

"You rushing off? You gonna tell your sister hello for us?" Mother asked.

"Yes, ma'am. Thanks for the coffee."

"Do you want to listen to my heart before you go?" Daddy asked, stalling. He hated for me to leave.

"Yes, sir," I replied.

He brought out the same old stethoscope and held out the ear-pieces to me. He pressed the diaphragm against the middle of his chest and looked at me with his good eye peering up, vulnerable, searching for some sign that I might disappear while he was watching me as hard as he could. After listening to the regular rhythm of his heart, I told him, "Your heart sounds good, Dad. I think you're in good shape."

"You really think so?"

"I really do," I said. He looked past me and saw himself in the pink-tinted mirror and grinned at his reflection. "Do you want me to get my shovel and come out and help you fill in the potholes?" He had already had his bath and he didn't want to, but he would have.

"No, sir. I'm working on my arms this afternoon."

"Your arms look perfectly fine to me."

"You love me. I always look good to you."

"That's right," he agreed. We hugged good-bye as if we might never see each other again. It was the way we said good-bye every day.

After filling my cart, I headed down the private dirt road. I saw Mary Ellen out in her swing, holding a cup of coffee on her knee. She's a tiny woman who can drink all the sugar she wants. She waved.

"Mother and Daddy say hello."

"Too busy to stop by today," she said, holding up her cup. "You want some? It's decaf."

I parked my cart alongside her swing. "Can always drink a cup of coffee," I replied honestly. "Uncle Tommy was here this afternoon."

"I saw him leave. Do you think he's happy?"

"I think so," I said.

"I saw him last week, and he didn't look right," Mary Ellen said as she walked slowly up the three steps to her front door. She stopped and looked across the land toward our parents' house. "Why do you suppose they built a house that big for just the two of them?"

"It's not just for them. It's for all of us."

"We have our own houses," she replied, and her eyes met mine and held my gaze. I shrugged.

"With or without sugar?" she asked.

"No sugar. I'm on a diet," I replied, staring off toward the dream house. I knew exactly what Mother and Daddy were doing. The evening news was just beginning, and they were having the conversation about why the four dogs Daddy had acquired needed to stay outdoors.

"You losing fast?" Mary Ellen asked.

"Nope. Dieting is the only thing I know that can stretch out time longer than . . ."

"Summer," she answered before going inside.

When she returned with my coffee, she brought her own fresh-ened cup, and we sat and slurped together. She tapped the ground with her foot, pushing us off in the swing. "You know we've been re-placed by those dogs, don't you?" she asked.

"Yes," I said. "The Incredible Hulk is you."

Mary Ellen grinned. When we were growing up, Daddy had al-ways called her "Mighty Mouse" because she was small but tough. "And Spot is Patty. Luke the Lab is Julie."

"And I'm Big Red. You know he stole those dogs from our neigh-bors, don't you?"

Mary Ellen nodded. "It would bother me if I didn't know how much he really likes dogs."

"He does," I agreed.

Her brow furrowed as if that was an idea that she needed to di-gest. "Time sure does go by fast," she said finally.

I thought it was a brilliant observation.

"Sure does. We better stop and enjoy it before we wake up dead."

The sky grew pinker, as it does just before night falls. Daddy's dogs had been yelping and then stopped because Mother finally relented and opened the back door to let them in. I could picture what would happen next. Spot and Hulk would hurriedly sit on either side of Daddy on the long green couch in the living room. Luke and Big Red would jump on the other orange sofa in the den by the fireplace that didn't work. Once the dogs were back inside keeping Daddy company, Mother would go upstairs to change into her nightgown. The water would run a long time before she finally came back down the stairs. As soon as her foot touched that top step, he would ask, "Lola, is that you?"

"Now who else would it be?" she always answered, coming slowly down the stairs. The dogs would rouse as if she were an intruder and then settle down again.

Dusk fell as Mary Ellen and I swung together in the tempo of summer. She and I saw the lights in the living room dim as Mother drew the drapes, and then the light from the television screen flick-ered behind them like firelight.

"Where's Steve?" I asked suddenly.

"Ball game," she replied.

"What kind of season is he having?" I inquired automatically.

My sister grinned widely, and then inhaled deeply as the breeze brought us a fresh whiff of tea olive. "He's Coach of the Year . . . again," she said with satisfaction.

Her foot continued to tap the ground, and we floated together in the twilight, waiting for the summer day to end.

From the Family Album . . .

The Legacy of a Very Handy Man

As I pedaled off on my bicycle to the post office, my daddy, who had just pumped up my tires with his own air compressor, called after me, "I hope you don't break down between here and there!"

It is just a two-mile ride to the post office, but no matter the distance I'm traveling or the current circumstances, that pessimistic parting shot is always my daddy's idea of a proper farewell: a doomsday good-bye. I can almost hear him praying behind my back whenever I leave him: "Lord, be merciful to that girl. There's no telling what could happen to her out there."

Dad's attitude is based on seventeen years of working the midnight shift as a troubleshooter for the local air-force base. Before that, he managed an apartment building. He also sold insurance. His work experience added up to a solid belief that the worst often happens, and so he devoted his life as a father to preparing his four daughters for the various afflictions and plagues he either remembers or can imagine.

They are considerable.

At age eleven, my oldest sister, Mary Ellen, was issued a small hatchet. She was in charge of it. It went under her side of the bed. Its purpose? To chop a hole through the bedroom window if the house caught on fire during the night and Dad wasn't there and Mom couldn't get to us. (Not to worry; Mom had her own hatchet.)

Dad's idea of a useful Christmas present one year was to give us girls each a can of shaving cream and a new safety razor. Another time, he gave us billfolds containing different-sized screwdrivers. No sexist, the next year he gave us portable sewing kits.

In our thirties now and having been exposed to most of Dad's survival sermonettes more than a few times, we are subjected to a subtle test-taking. Dad does it very cagily, but the underlying question is always the same: Are his girls going to prove to be good Boy Scouts — always prepared for the nasty surprises that life has to offer? By our preparedness we will justify his life's work as a father.

At the annual lighting of my furnace, on the very day before cold weather is predicted, Dad shows up early in the morning, refuses my stall of an offer of freshly brewed coffee, and asks me, "Where are your matches, your flashlight, and a nine-inch candle?"

Like a nurse assisting in surgery, I pull these items from a drawer next to the room where he'll be working.

Dad smiles. He is a fulfilled father in that moment. But the glow doesn't last.

The door to the heating unit sticks. "When's the last time you oiled these hinges?" The question is accusatory. I shrug and answer him with a question. "Last year? About this time?" I'm not into hinges.

"WD-40," he demands, shaking his head. I'm off to the kitchen, where I find my can of WD-40 hiding underneath the sink, camouflaged by a pile of old rags. I leave the door ajar, hoping that Dad will spy those old rags — he loves them so.

"I don't suppose you have the straw that comes with it," he says, his voice changing. He is preparing to be disappointed. "It helps to aim the lubricant if you have that straw."

Smugly, I fondle the tiny plastic straw, pulling it gently free from the inch of tape I've used to secure it to the can. Our eyes meet, and he nods approvingly. It is a sweet moment of pleasing a parent.

For there are too many times when I feel like a disappointment as a daughter not to have exercised more of what I have learned from Dad. Living next door to him, I find it temptingly easy to call him up for favors rather than do a job myself. It's not like I don't know what to do. I have been listening to his survival lessons for over thirty years now, and I can prove it.

Here are a few of Dad's tips, just as he told them to me.

- Always open the nozzle of a garden hose again to relieve the pressure after turning off the faucet. The water pressure can build up from a residual drip and burst your hose.
- Carry a jug of water in the car. You never know when you'll break down on the road. A person can live for days without food, but for only seventy-two hours without water.
- If you smell escaping gas in a room, open the window immediately and unplug the telephone. A spark from a ringing telephone can set off a gas fire.
- There's hardly anything in the world that doesn't work better if you put a little grease on it. It's grease, not love, that makes the world go round.

In addition to the litany of survival rules, Dad offered this standard advice for gift-giving: "Honey, when you need to buy a present for a man for his birthday or any other occasion, don't buy him a shirt or a tie. Show him you've got some sense. Go to the hardware store and buy him a big roll of silver duct tape. There's not a man alive who doesn't want a big roll of that."

5

Private Road

"Your daddy's heart is out of rhythm," Mother whispered into the phone.

"I'll be right over," I said, taking a deep breath. I turned off my computer and headed down the private road. On the other side of the ditch that separated our acreage from the nearby subdivision, our neighbor's fancy new silver-haired dog barked a blue streak at me as I went by, and I barked back, "Quiet down, you loud, worrisome mutt!"

He was anything but a mutt. Unlike my Daddy's four dogs, this pedigreed pooch was bought with the money my daddy had paid our neighbor after the man's flock of peacocks had supposedly dropped dead from fright after being lethally barked at by Daddy's dogs.

Unwilling to argue over other possible and more logical causes of the birds' sudden deaths, Daddy accepted the neighbor's verdict and paid him off, only to have his good money used to purchase a fancy dog that was introduced proudly by the owner. "This dog don't bark. If he ever looks like he's going to make any noise, I just tell him to be quiet, and he shuts right up."

I had watched Daddy's face while he listened to our neighbor's ridiculous boast, and his expression didn't change. Daddy simply nodded, patted the blueblood on his silver head, and walked back down the private road to his home and to his own mixed-breed dogs, which whooped enthusiastically upon his return. They were a motley crew of goofy-looking animals he had enticed from the homes of neighbors who lived on his daily walking route.

Espying thirsty or hungry animals whose owners were at work, Daddy stopped and filled water bowls and handed out dog kibble. As a result of what he considered a ministry of mercy, four of the dogs had followed him home. We all thought this was funny, but he didn't like to be teased about stealing our neighbors' dogs or questioned about what we called the Peacock Incident, either.

Mother opened the front door, looking over my shoulder down the road where the neighbor's dog was still barking. Our eyes connected.

"Yeah, he never barks," I said, as she held open the door.

Daddy was sitting on the long green sofa with the stethoscope plugged into his ears. "I think my heart's fine, but your mother says it's out of rhythm." He handed me the earpieces.

I placed the diaphragm on his chest and listened. Usually the heartbeat sounded fine, but today it was fast. It did sound irregular. I placed my hand on Daddy's forehead. He closed his eyes, as if he needed to black out the knowledge that it was beginning again — this business with his heart. His skin felt clammy. "Let's call the doctor," I said.

Mother nodded, went to the kitchen, and punched in the familiar number. I heard her recounting Daddy's usual symptoms. The answer didn't take long. "They want him to check in this afternoon at four o'clock. They'll try the pills tonight, and if that doesn't work . . ."

"They'll jump-start me tomorrow," Daddy said tiredly, as if I didn't know the procedure. "Maybe it'll straighten out tonight."

Probably wouldn't. It usually didn't.

I plopped down on Mother's rocker, the chair her own daddy had sat in and which she inherited after he died. I placed my hands on the wooden armrests where Pa's hands used to be and took a deep breath.

"You don't need to worry about me," Daddy said, crossing his arms over his chest. He began to whistle nervously a series of birdcalls that made his dogs yelp. Mother got up and went to the back door. "You boys get on out of here."

Daddy's dogs reluctantly left him, their tails down as they obeyed Mother's command. Daddy looked forlorn. He was watching the muted television intently.

"You stay with your daddy," Mother said. "I need to go upstairs for a few minutes."

"Will you be gone long?" Daddy asked, his gaze still fixed on the silent TV. Mother walked up the stairs without answering him.

I heard the door to their bedroom close. I tapped the audio button on the remote, and we watched an *Andy Griffith* rerun, the episode about Aunt Bea's homemade pickles, which we both knew by heart.

"That's always a good show," Daddy said when the credits began to roll.

I nodded. Life in Mayberry was picturesque. As if on cue, the sound of water running upstairs suddenly stopped. Daddy turned his head toward the wall-sized mirror opposite the stairway which showed everything that happened behind him. He had installed it, he said, to make the big living room look even bigger. I heard Mother's movements before her right foot took that first step. The minute she was visible in the mirror, Daddy let out the longest wolf whistle any man could make in praise of a woman's allure.

I winced.

Mother hated that sound. When he first started the whistling, Mother asked him to stop it, and he laughed. She asked him again real nice, but he didn't seem to hear her. Then she asked him solemnly to quit, and he laughed again. Daddy knew the whistle made her mad, but he simply couldn't stop himself.

The smell of hairspray and Oscar de la Renta returned with mother. Seeing me still on the couch, she acted surprised that I was still there, although she had told me to stay. "You better go on home. Be back at 3:30 to drive your daddy to the hospital."

I nodded, surprised by the sudden dismissal. Mother took my place in Pa's chair after I stood up. I leaned over to hug Daddy, who closed his eyes again, as if my embrace was part of the sequence of events dealing with his heart that he needed to steel himself against. The two of them fastened their eyes upon the TV screen. When I stopped at the pink-tinted mirror by the front door and waited for my parents to say good-bye, I could see their reflections, but they were already engrossed in a rerun of *Bewitched*.

The blueblood was still patrolling the fence of his own back yard, and when he barked again to announce my presence, I declared loud enough for his owner to hear me, "If I were a peacock, I'd be dead by now!"

"Who are you yelling at?" Mary Ellen asked, rising suddenly from where she had been lying supine in a bed of purple tulips.

I walked across the field to where she lay and fell down beside her.

"Everything okay?" she asked.

"Daddy's heart is out of rhythm again."

"I thought it was about time for that," she said enigmatically, and then she began to hum.

"I remember that song — sort of. What is it?"

She hummed a bit more and then sang the lyric: *"The moon is a harsh mistress. It's hard to love her well."*

When she finished, I asked her, "Do you think there is something wrong with us for not moving away from our parents?"

"We love our family. There's nothing wrong with that," Mary Ellen stated flatly. But an opaqueness entered her gaze, and I knew that my sister had places within herself that her family was not allowed.

"I've been thinking about your dream," she said, stretching out her legs. They were short and defiantly muscular. She was referring to my most recent dream about living in a rehabilitation center. Mary Ellen and I often discussed my dreams. She was an English teacher and very good at deciphering symbolism.

"I think the key to understanding this dream is the matron. The matron is God," Mary Ellen declared.

"That's possible. And the little stranger in the mirror? Who is that?" I could still remember my heart's impression of a dream child whose likeness was caught beside me in the mirror. The little thing was stooped over, bent in half, giving the appearance of not being completely formed.

"That child could be anybody, really. The size indicates that it could even represent me." Mary Ellen tendered her idea as if self-conscious about suggesting that she was an interloper in my subconscious.

"A possible explanation," I admitted. "Or it could be Julie Ann or Patty Kate, for they are younger, and youth often associates itself with size." I did have Patty Kate on my mind a lot. She had relocated with her new husband to the Florida Keys and was not very communicative — a bad sign. "Do you think Daddy retired too soon?" I asked, suddenly distracted. "He's so restless."

"He's driving Mother crazy," Mary Ellen said bluntly. "It's a wonder she hasn't killed him."

"Following someone around the house night and day isn't grounds for justifiable homicide."

"The jury wouldn't buy self-defense?" she proposed.

I laughed softly. "He doesn't let Mother go to the bathroom without asking how long she'll be gone."

"He watches all of us," she said solemnly.

My sister and I stared into each other's eyes for some clue as to what was happening to the man who had raised us to have walking-around sense. Mary Ellen blinked first, and when she did, she changed the subject. "I have big news."

I waited.

"Patty Kate is pregnant. She's coming home."

"To live with Mother and Daddy?" I asked stupidly.

Mary Ellen nodded seriously. "The marriage isn't working out."

Grief assaulted me in that moment. Grief for my younger sister's disappointments. Grief for my daddy's heart condition and growing list of eccentricities. Grief for my mother's confinement. Grief for Mary Ellen, who challenged the harsh moon with her singing.

"How is Patty doing?" I asked.

"We'll see when she gets here. She's going to have the baby down there, and then bring her home."

"So it's a girl," I said dully.

Mary Ellen nodded. "She had a sonogram. Patty always wanted a baby. Her clock was ticking."

"All our clocks are ticking," I sighed, pushing myself up. There were words to be written.

Accustomed to my sudden shifts of attention, she asked, "When are you going to let me see some of your new book?"

Our eyes met, and I wanted to tell her everything: that I was writing about the creation-versus-evolution trial, and that Clarence Darrow was not the hero people thought he was, and that William Jennings Bryan had been unable to explain how the Bible was different from other books in his testimony on the stand. But how could I explain all that when I hadn't been able to get it right in 900 pages? I shrugged.

Mary Ellen read my inner struggle, and her eyes filled with compassion. I saw her want to say something encouraging about having a family of my own, about having a baby, about Daddy. But all she could say was, "I'm going to make some grape jelly soon."

Her grape jelly was pure and perfectly sweet and so fresh that grocery-store jam was like a whole different food. It was something to look forward to.

"Two jars?" I requested as I headed across the field of tall grass and wildflowers. The blueberry bush was flourishing, and I wondered if I could make time later to pick and freeze some. My mind toyed with other escapes from work and heart problems until I was back inside my house. I put on a pot of coffee, and from my kitchen window I looked out at my sister, who fell over on her back so that the sun could shine on her face. Her clear soprano tones drifted my way. She sang her song for Patty Kate, for Daddy, for Mother. Mary Ellen sang a song for us all.

"*Once the sun did shine. Good Lord, it felt so fine. The moon, a phantom rose, through the mountains and the pines. And then the darkness fell. The moon is a harsh mistress. It's hard to love her well.*"

A part of me moved back across the field and abided with my sister while she lay in the grass. The dog next door barked on and on, and I wondered if Daddy could hear him. Settling down, I did not turn immediately to working on my book, which I called "The Prayer-maker."

Instead, I decided to polish a draft of an essay I wrote about the last time I took Dad in for a tune-up.

From the Family Album . . .

An Evening Sky

"Look at the hawk up there," he says as we drive on the interstate that will take us to the hospital. "He's gonna catch something soon. He's ready."

Feigning interest, I crane my neck to see the great hawk perched high up on a limb of a tall tree. I envy his distant position, so removed from danger down here.

As we pass over the Alabama River, Dad comments, "I've been thinking I'm going to drop that flood insurance. We didn't get flooded out last year. It would have to be one big rain to get us."

Since we live on the flood plain, Dad speaks of flood insurance often, vacillating between wanting it and hoping he won't need it.

At the hospital, admission is routine. This trip is our fifth in two years to take Dad in for what he calls "a tune-up." His room is a large, sunny one, but his bed is too high to climb into. Casually we circle the bed, trying to find a button to push to lower it. The doctor comes in before we can find it.

One more time, while we are all standing, the doctor goes over the treatment plan: heart monitor, IV, jump-start tomorrow at one o'clock if the chemicals fail to re-establish a regular heartbeat. I listen mutely, praying silently: "Please, God, don't let me see burn marks on my father's chest again."

"The nurse will help you with the bed," the doctor promises, as if he's nervous that I will ask him to perform this simple task. I won't —

for the same reason that I wouldn't ask him to change a burned-out lightbulb. I don't want to know for certain what his limitations are.

When he's gone, my father grins and says, "He is married."

"I didn't notice," I sniff.

"You women like to pretend you don't look to see whether a man is married or not, but you look."

"What's it to you?" I ask. We are thwarted in our usual bantering by the arrival of a maintenance man who has been sent to fix the bed. He leans over, presses the correct button, and the bed goes down. As he leaves, the handyman gives my dad a thumbs-up.

"Now there's a doctor!" Dad approves.

"He is married," I say. It takes my father a moment, but then he chuckles. Our tension eases.

Maybe the chemicals will work just like that button on the bed. Maybe they won't have to do the electric-paddle treatment. I'm just about to let myself start hoping for the best when the nurse comes in and tells Dad to undress.

It begins again.

Dad doesn't like for me to see him without his shirt, so I kiss him good-bye and leave the room. My throat constricts when I pass the nurses' station. "That's my daddy you've got in room 323."

"We'll give him back to you in good shape," a nurse promises.

I nod as if we have a contract. In the car, I head toward home, a distant place not as inviting to me now as that tree where the great hawk still sits high up, watching the world beneath him. The sight of him consoles me. He reminds me of the father I grew up with: poised and strong, ever watching the world to make sure it ran right. I keep the bird in my sights for as long as I can.

6

Can You Hear Me, Brother Woodrow?

"Why does that fellow on the TV keep asking, 'Are you ready, Brother Woodrow?'"

All of us sitting in the living room turn to Daddy and look at him as if he were crazy. In my family, this response is the way we keep one another from going over the edge. We glare at goofy behavior and follow up this discipline with ribbing and jibes. In a family as large as ours, this is almost a full-time occupation. One of us is always going kind of crazy.

"That's Hank Williams Jr. on the TV, and he isn't saying, 'Are you ready, Brother Woodrow?' He's saying, 'Are you ready for some football?' It's Monday night. Monday-night football. Get it?" I explain.

"I wish they would get someone who could talk plain. I don't even like the way Hank Jr. sings," Daddy grumbles.

We turn up the TV so Dad can hear. Hank Jr. comes on again in a few minutes, and this time, Daddy repeats the correct words with him.

One by one, we can't help it — we start to laugh.

Mother turns to Daddy and asks, "Are you ready for some popcorn, Brother Woodrow?"

More laughter. For the rest of the evening, we tease Daddy about getting hard of hearing by asking, "Are you ready, Brother Woodrow?"

He takes it, this teasing. Maybe too well. Underneath all this tomfoolery, we are seriously trying to tell him that he has some kind of hearing problem. So far, he hasn't heard any of us when we've tried to hint that his ears aren't what they used to be.

I pretend to just think of this bright idea. I say, "Hey, Brother Woodrow, why don't you let me call the Speech and Hearing Clinic over at the college in the morning and see what they charge for an exam?"

Because he is the center of attention, Dad shrugs good-naturedly: Okay, why not?

I have been trying to work up to making this suggestion for weeks, and it was just that easy.

I call the AUM clinic in the morning. I learn that my father is not unusual at all. Most people will admit to almost any physical failing except deafness. I learn that deafness can happen to anybody, young or old. Ninety percent of the cases can be corrected.

Jubilantly, I call Dad to tell him that I can get him an appointment next Friday. I soft-soap him: "Whaddya say, Brother Woodrow? I'll even buy you lunch."

He is not charmed by my proposal. He is a different man today. "Do you really think I need to get my hearing checked? I know it has probably slipped a little, but I can hear pretty good." His voice is sharp-edged. He is not inviting teasing this morning. "Tell me honestly: Do you really think I need to see a doctor?"

I gulp. This opportunity to get him some help is no time for feminine tact. "Daddy, I've been standing right behind you talking, and you don't hear me."

"Are you joking?"

"No, sir. I am not."

On the phone, we move from being buddies to that miserable plane of existence called role reversal. Increasingly, my thirty-something friends report the same tension: aging parent ignores the changes of his body, forcing a child to assume a parental role.

Simultaneously, I grow angry with this man I adore when I let myself think about how he is putting off correcting his hearing loss. This mulish response is so unlike the man I know. He's the guy who brought home an eye chart when I was nine years old and figured out that I was flunking in school because I couldn't see. For weeks while failing in school, I had lived a tortured existence of self-questioning. I thought I was stupid because my test grades were constantly proving that I was. Then Daddy showed me what was wrong by asking me to read some letters from across the room. I was so relieved and embarrassed to be named nearsighted instead of dumb that I screamed and locked myself in the bathroom.

In that bathroom, alone, I stuffed a washrag in my mouth to muffle my crying while I looked at my eyes in the mirror and wondered why they had gone bad on me. I figure Daddy has known a few confused moments when he's studied his reflection and wondered why it no longer conforms to the image he has of himself as our protector.

Oh, Daddy.

I hang up the phone and pick it right back up. I call Julie Ann. She answers on the first ring.

"He's changed his mind about going to the hearing clinic," I say, sighing.

"You bragged on him too soon," Julie assesses.

"I don't know what to do next. I want you to encourage Mother to stay on his case."

"I hear her yelling at him when she's on the phone to me."

"He has taken to tuning her out."

"That's one of the problems. We don't know how much of this is him tuning us all out and how much is ear trouble," Julie Ann theorizes.

"Or he might just need to have his ears cleaned. It could be that simple," I suggest optimistically.

"We'll work on him. We'll get his bones over there. You're doing the right thing. Keep it up," Julie Ann encourages.

Words help. I need her understanding that I am not being presumptuous. And a nag. Underneath it all, I'm afraid that if I'm the one to convince Daddy there's something wrong with him, he may not like me as much anymore.

Later that day, I wander over to Mother and Daddy's for afternoon coffee. Matthew, Mary Ellen's youngest son, comes in from school right after I get there.

"How you doing, Pa?" Matt speaks loudly. He's learned that he'd better. He's gotten in trouble more than once for supposedly not saying hello or good-bye when he comes and goes around here.

"There's an orange drink in the refrigerator for you, son," Dad tells him.

As Matthew moves around the kitchen assembling his snack, he tells us the details of his day. He mentions the bus ride, the amount of homework he has to do. He sits down next to his grandfather.

"Son, how was your day?" Dad asks.

Matthew looks at me and rolls his eyes. "Pa, you're getting as deaf as some old man. I just told you all about my day."

Daddy looks at me to see if Matt is playing some kind of childish trick on him. Anxiety attacks me. I am torn between sparing my father's feelings and protecting Matthew, who is innocent here.

"Matthew just told us that he had a good day, but he's got a lot of homework," I say loudly. "You didn't hear him."

Daddy rises up like we've conspired against him, goes into the living room, and gets on the couch with his dog Spot. He turns up the TV. We shuffle in after him. He scans the TV channels. "I can hear that," he declares, stopping at Headline News. "I can hear that. And that. I don't think my hearing's so bad."

"Daddy, I fell off my bike the other day while you were getting in your mail. I screamed for you to help me, and you didn't hear me." I had not meant to tell him that.

He looks confused by what I've said. Dejected. On the verge of being defeated. And I am responsible. I shouldn't be saying these cruel words to my father, but I cannot stop talking. "What if Mother were to fall down?"

"Your mother never falls down."

Matthew, bored with the conversation, gets up.

"You leaving, son?"

Daddy doesn't hear Matt say good-bye. I go over and hug Dad and tell him I'm going to break his bones if he doesn't let me take him in to get his hearing checked. Mother, who's just come into the room, laughs softly, as if she knows a secret. "You still working on your daddy?"

"Yeah, but Brother Woodrow won't listen to me today."

"He'll get around to hearing you," she predicts enigmatically.

I stand behind my father and pull on the lobes of his ears, threatening other catastrophes if he doesn't do what is good for him. He sits in front of me, holding the remote control for the TV, scanning the channels, tuning in and out randomly.

Later, Daddy doesn't hear me either when I say good-bye.

From the Family Album . . .

Across the Creek from Luckytown

He is coming from the far back corner of our property. Head up, he is wearing the same white T-shirt and jeans he's worn ever since I can remember. His posture is military perfect as he scans the woods like a scout. He is blind in one eye, so he must turn his head fully to compensate for restricted peripheral vision. Periodically he claps his hands: 1-2-3. He is paging his dogs.

It embarrasses Daddy when his dogs go off looking for love. "They're making fools of themselves," he says.

It is very early in the morning, and I am not dressed. I hurriedly pull on my sneakers and run out in my nightgown to help my father look for Spot, the smallest dog. "Is something wrong?" I call out.

He cups his hand around the ear next to his blind eye.

I yell louder. "Is something wrong?"

He squints as if he doesn't recognize me, and I stop in that moment and wait for him to figure out that I am not a ghost. Finally, he nods.

I know something is wrong. Dad is afraid. It's happening more and more often, this coming of fear. Today, Dad fears that something bad has happened to Spot. I know this instinctively because Daddy is coming from the direction of our property where the bad things happen. That back left corner of the woods is where the Incredible Hulk, Dad's other favorite dog, was bitten by a snake last year.

I went with Dad to find the Hulk, a black, sausage-shaped dog that could only finish dying after Daddy got out his gun. Those three shots ring in my memory now: bam-bam-bam.

Silently we trail the creek, which is where our small city has laid the new sewage lines. They have torn up our trees, savaged the natural terrain that gave us the illusion that nothing bad could happen in our neck of the woods. Next door, across the creek in Luckytown, is where the bad things are supposed to happen. Inside these boundaries is where we live.

"Spot!" My father's hands make the sound of a gun: clap-clap-clap.

I hear for the first time the resemblance to the death knell he sounded over Hulk, Spot's mother. Why three shots? I wondered then. Why not just one bullet to stop the slow death of snake venom? One shot would have done it. Now I hear very clearly that Dad sent Hulk off with the same signal that he used to call her. Three shots, three claps: I love you.

While I watch him, he looks for a long moment across the creek. Private planes with cargoes of cocaine are rumored to land there. Not so long ago his old friend Buddy was found shot to death in his pickup truck there. It was a suicide staged as a drug-related murder, said the police. Others said that Buddy got cancer, grew depressed, and pulled the trigger. Dad thinks of his friend, but he doesn't want to remember Buddy dying that way. He pushes the memory away as we press forward. The tall, damp grass slaps against my bare legs.

Daddy is oblivious to my attire or discomfort. He is looking for his dogs, though they are not really lost. Still, he is searching, straining to listen, only he can't hear so well, and what he does hear he doesn't always trust. As I watch him, I catalogue his behaviors, his other physical problems. He has dizzy spells. And he has lost weight since his heart developed an erratic beat. The medicine he takes makes little red sore places on the insides of his arms that look like needle tracks. I avert my eyes from the evidence of the toxic substance that circulates now in his bloodstream.

I call, "I saw Spot earlier while I was drinking my first cup of coffee. He's not lost — he's just in love."

This time, Daddy really doesn't hear me. I've been trying to tell him ten different ways that his hearing's gone bad on him, and ten different times he has ignored me. He's putting off acknowledging growing deaf. Growing old.

It is my job to clap my hands until he hears me. This is something we can fix, I want to tell him. You got me glasses when I was nine years old. I was flunking out in school, and no one could understand why. You laughed out loud when you discovered that I wasn't dumb, just blind. I forgave you that humiliation — that day you laughed at me. Now I'm going to get your ears checked and get you a hearing aid, and you will forgive me for being the one to do it. It's that simple. This is change, but it's not desperate change. We don't have to get the gun for this.

Brave talk. So grown-up. But I don't like it. That's my daddy who can't hear what I'm saying.

Once more his gaze sweeps the overgrown field. I hike my nightgown up around my knees. We are silent trackers together.

Suddenly I hear barking. Daddy doesn't. "See? See Spot run!" I cry out. It would be a funny joke if he could hear me. Just that quick, I am impatient with him. It's his own fault that his relief and joy are delayed. I give him a moment to wonder what I'm saying, and then I yell some more and point. His good eye is watering profusely in sympathy with his blind eye, but he is able to see his dogs. They are coming to him. Only three of them now.

"They're all right," he whispers to himself. He seems surprised that they are safe, that nothing bad has happened today. This hurts me. Have pain and fear become such a part of his life that good news is the exception?

Rubbing their heads, examining them with his fingers for wounds and ticks, Dad complains, "You boys just make complete fools of yourselves."

He leaves me without saying good-bye. I am a little wounded by his forgetting me so easily, but my own pain is salved by watching him as he walks away. The sun shines on him and his white T-shirt. From this distance, I cannot tell he is blind in one eye. His military posture belies the truth that he has arthritis in his spine. His dogs bound and bark around him, and he is smiling as if he can hear them. His pleasure in his dogs gives me unequaled joy.

"Everything is going to be all right," I promise from an ever-growing distance that old man who has become my father. I hope it's the truth, but he is no longer the hero of my youth, and I do not know for sure.

7

A Stolen Life

Before I could reach for the doorknob and let myself in for afternoon coffee, Daddy jerked the front door open and reported the bad news loudly, as if I was the one with a hearing problem. "We've been robbed!"

Mother was sitting in her easy chair in the living room, staring at the television, which was never turned off anymore. The mute button had been pressed again, so the picture flitted by without sound. She didn't seem to notice. Charlton Heston was playing Moses in *The Ten Commandments*. He was about to part the Red Sea.

"Your daddy's coin collection is missing," Mother said, her voice deadly.

"All of them?"

Daddy grew flustered. He began to flap his arms excitedly while he paced the room. I feared that if he kept up all this activity, he was likely to throw his heart out of whack. I sat down, hoping that by remaining still I could encourage him to be less excitable.

"No. Not all of them. I've still got the half-dollars and the two-dollar bills. But the sack of bicentennial quarters is gone."

"Have you looked for them very carefully?"

He became exasperated. "I know where I left my coins!"

"They were in the safe in your office?"

"Of course not. I only keep important papers in the safe, not money. I hid the coins in the file cabinet."

"Under the 'M'?" I asked dourly.

It bothered me that Daddy kept an expensive safe in his office, but he left the door to it ajar and a note on the front with the combination printed on it and this message: *The contents of this safe are for record-keeping purposes only. There's nothing valuable inside to steal. If you don't take my word for it, and the door has gotten shut, here's the combination. Look for yourself.* Daddy was trusting that a potential burglar would also be literate.

The safe was a precaution against fire or flood damage. We lived on the flood plain, and Daddy was always worried about the Alabama River backing up in our yard and drowning our houses and the records of his real-estate deals.

"Mother, have you looked too?"

She didn't answer. Her expression was grim. "Your daddy knows where he left his quarters."

"Is anything else gone? How did the person break in? What did the police say?"

"No one broke in, and we aren't calling the police," Mother reported glumly.

"All things considered, it had to be an inside job," Daddy theorized, his jaw working.

"What?" Understanding began to dawn. "Do you think I took them?" I asked, incredulous.

"Of course not. We know who took them. We know it wasn't you," Daddy said.

Mother rose and went to the kitchen. When she returned, she was holding a cup of coffee for me and a plate of oatmeal cookies, my favorite kind.

"What I don't understand is that the boy knows he can have anything I've got. Matthew didn't have to steal them. I would have given them to him if he wanted them."

"You think Matthew took your sack of quarters?"

"I don't think it. I know it!" Daddy declared, settling onto the sofa. When Mother offered him the plate of cookies, he took three. "I love these things," he said, munching, suddenly content. It struck me as

peculiar. The center of attention now, Daddy seemed to relax, like a
child who had pitched a tantrum and gotten his way.

He wasn't making sense. He should be remembering that verse
from the Bible that urges if someone steals something, let him have it
— that verse. As I had aged, I had not grown any better at memorizing
Scripture, but I thought I had taken the spirit of the Bible's message of
love into my heart. I thought Daddy had too. Yet this concern over his
missing money and his accusations were about to divide our family.
Oblivious to the danger, Daddy was eating oatmeal cookies.

"How do you know Matthew took them?" I asked cautiously.

"Your daddy says that Matthew was curious about them, and he
was the only person he had shown where they were hidden," Mother
explained impatiently. She took a deep breath and blew out the air —
a nervous habit she had picked up since Daddy retired.

"The boy could have had them or anything else I owned. He didn't
have to steal them. I'm going down there and tell him that just as soon
as I've finished my snack. Your mother didn't make us a real lunch today. Just soup." His voice was acquiring a whine that jarred with the
nature of the man I had grown up with: the man who had claimed he
could eat a can of Vienna sausages for a meal and be happy.

"Let me take another look upstairs before you do anything," I said.

As if my request were a dare, Daddy rose and strode determinedly
across the living room and out the front door to walk down our private dirt road to his other daughter's house. I wanted to call Mary Ellen and warn her — to tell her to hide in the house and not listen to
anything Daddy said.

"Mother, did you search the filing cabinet too? Did you check his
desk? It's like a rat's nest up there. Sometimes a different set of eyes
can see what someone else can't."

"Your daddy knows where he keeps his coins," Mother repeated
tiredly. She had lived long enough to know that sometimes hard
truths must simply be accepted. She tapped the mute button off on the
TV when the phrase "Special News Alert" appeared on the screen. We
both waited to see what was important enough to interrupt our regularly scheduled program, but it was only one more repeat of the same

old tape where President Reagan kept saying he couldn't recall certain facts about the Iran-Contra affair. Every time something else happened in the investigation, they ran that tape.

"I wish they would leave Reagan alone. How do they expect one man to remember everything?" Mother mused softly.

Daddy returned from his mission, arms still flapping at his sides, his face red. "Mary Ellen is mad as a hornet. But the child will get over it. Matthew denied everything, naturally. So he's a liar too. I hated to do it, but you have to nip this kind of behavior in the bud, or it will end worse than me being disappointed in a grandson."

"It was hard, but it had to be done," Mother said, resigned. She sounded foreign and older than she had been just an hour ago. Then, suddenly straightening, she pulled back her shoulders and declared, "You can't let these things ride. I don't ever want to be visiting a grandson of mine in jail."

"Matthew isn't like that," I said. Inside, a part of me splintered, moving away from the comfortable ritual of afternoon coffee with my parents, who were wounded but determined to face this new trouble head-on. Had Daddy called his oldest daughter a child? Didn't he know that Mary Ellen was an adult woman with opaqueness in her eyes and secrets that had nothing to do with him? I worried about my sister. There were times when she seemed only to watch herself live rather than be present in her life. The doctors called it depression.

"Some things you can't see at first," Mother said. "But the signs are there."

"How can you really know that Matthew took the coins?" I persisted.

"Your daddy knows what he knows, and I know what I know," Mother explained. They were irritated with what sounded to them like disrespect.

"I'm going home," I said. I don't think I had ever said that before. Home had always been wherever my parents lived. Down the road was just my house.

Neither of them offered me a second cookie or a refill on my coffee, and I recalled another verse from the Bible that warned people not to go into the homes of their neighbors too often because folks can grow tired of frequent visitors. For the first time in my life, I wondered if I had overstayed my welcome with my parents. It was a new idea for me — one that the nature of their love had never permitted before. But that afternoon, family love had mutated into an affair of the heart that allowed one of us to accuse the other of stealing coins that were not worth more than their face value.

Didn't Daddy know that? Bicentennial quarters were mixed with copper. They had no more value than any other kind of quarter, and I didn't predict they ever would. Daddy collected them because he had a fascination with money that had grown during his days home with Mother. And now, over twenty dollars in quarters, we were splitting up. It didn't make sense.

I walked the familiar dirt road home. Mary Ellen wasn't outside today. Her drapes were drawn. If she had hung a sign on the front door that read "No Salesmen Allowed," the message could not have been plainer. She didn't want me coming in there and trying to sell her on the idea that our parents would repent — come to their senses — or that everything was all right. Nothing was all right.

I understood my sister's wounded position, but I was offended by the silence from her home. For I was not my parents, and I had not accused Matthew of stealing Daddy's money. Inside my own house, I too drew my drapes and pretended that I wasn't home.

I kept working on my book, "The Prayermaker." I finally finished it, but I didn't like how the story ended. Like William Jennings Bryan, I was ultimately unable to explain to people like Clarence Darrow how justice meets grace in the Word. I shoved the manuscript under my bed and decided to take some time out from being a writer of fiction to work on a master's degree in liberal arts. I had run into an old college professor of mine, Dr. Ben Williams, and after a five-minute conversation with him, I was reminded how much I loved studying literature. How could I have forgotten?

Within a couple of weeks I was enrolled in graduate school and started my first class. Within a year, I finished all the course work and pared down what could have been a four-hundred-page thesis to a two-hundred-page volume of personal essays about family life. I named it "Living with Strangers." And when I was ultimately scheduled to present and defend my thesis to the academic body of the university, no one in my family attended, though "Living with Strangers" was largely about them.

From the Family Album . . .

Living on the Flood Plain

In the year of the tornado and the hurricane and the blizzard, my father began a fresh lament. "Our land is on the hundred-year flood plain," he announced. "We all need to take out flood insurance."

Ten years ago, no one in the family took Dad's fearfulness seriously, mostly because his news flash was indiscernible in its delivery from his other predictions of bad times, which he has given his days over to proclaiming. My father has, in his mid-sixties, become the black cloud that he claims he was born under.

Every day he predicts disaster ahead. Every day he sees an omen, feels a tremor of evil, cautions us that he is not long for this world because "Something isn't right." Implicit in this last foretelling of his own death is the threat that he and his prophecies of doom are the dam holding back the crushing flood of multitudinous distresses that will fall upon us once he is no longer here to worry about them.

I do not tell him that his words of worry have lost their ability to alarm me. To move me toward some act of self-defense. Mostly I have become inured to his prophecies, discounting them as one does Chicken Little's pronouncements that the sky is falling.

When Daddy feels that we are tuning him out, he listens to Headline News and recounts to us the reports of tornadoes, hurricanes, floods, and blizzards. Or he calls the InfoLine to hear about natural disasters that are happening around the world even as he holds the phone and listens.

His worst suspicions confirmed, he makes another contribution to the Red Cross, as if this sacrifice of money to the people who clean up after natural disasters might somehow prevent these acts of God from happening to him. To us.

I sense that in these acts of sacrifice and warning my father is trying to negotiate with Fate itself, trying to redirect the course of the future as one might the course of a swollen river that is presently headed toward a populous area. That is, where we live.

I live in a house next door to Dad on a parcel of land that is not particularly desirable. It is boggy terrain — swampland, really. We are wedded not to the land called the flood plain but to the people of our blood, attempting to do what feels at times unimaginable — to love each other well as we grow older.

Does it sound peculiar — the hope of loving well? It is not a capitalist ambition. Not a politically correct one. Psychiatrists have little good to say about girls who still love their fathers. I have no defense. I offer no excuse. I love my family, my father.

At times, it isn't easy. Old age and fear make nervous neighbors, and my daddy, who boasts of failing daily, does not resemble the hero of my youth, who promised that incomparable brand of security called paternal protection. Instead of fighting growing older, he appears to fall in love with the drama of ailing, with his symptoms, with doctors and pills.

Out of this winter romance, he gives up his job of being his daughter's hero. His wife's lover. His attention is directed not toward protecting and saving but toward predicting disaster. "I told you so" becomes his motto. He is no longer Atlas holding up the world. In old age, my father shrugs. It is an unexpected betrayal — this retirement from his post as the family protector.

His neighbors — his children — do not know what to say to this man. Finally, though we are half his age and do not expect the waters to come, we buy the flood insurance to give him peace of mind, and even that is not enough to bring stability to a relationship that has not always been peaceful. But there has been in it an equanimity, an understanding that no matter what happens, we will be together as a family. Only togetherness is no longer axiomatic. We are headed toward separation.

It is this despair that we will part that overshadows the daily love of being together — feels like the boulder Sisyphus pushed up a hill. Every day is not progress — not time gained and enjoyed together but time lost. The future is not ahead. It is being stolen, not by death but by the man who is fearfully living it.

I wonder if there is anything an ex-hero's child can do to redirect the course of her father's life. What act will be god-sized enough to rewrite the content of a man's daily speech, change the way he feels about himself and what is happening in this natural act of God known as growing older?

My sister Julie saw the aftermath of a tornado that killed ten people. "You have to see it to absorb the reality of the power. We only lived a mile away, and it didn't touch us. But it could have. It left me feeling — I don't know — solemn."

I have not seen a homesite robbed of its dwelling by a force of nature like a tornado or a flood, but I have lived beside my father as he grew older; and I too am left with an alliance with survivors, and like my sister, I feel solemn.

8

The Mother Load

After Uncle Tommy died, the mantel clock that had been snuffling along through the years, still muffled, died too. Daddy didn't try to fix it. He went out and bought one of those big, old-fashioned brown schoolhouse clocks and placed it high over the kitchen counter.

It was exactly the same kind of clock that an anonymous person at my church had hung on the wall opposite the pulpit during a season of guest speakers coming in to fill the void left by our preacher, who moved out to California. Everyone in the congregation saw the clock first thing Sunday morning at the same time and understood the implications. Preachers need to be able to tell time.

But a sensitive soul who said that preachers didn't need to look time so squarely in the face took it down and hung it in the church kitchen, where we didn't really need it. That's where it stayed, however, and it looked about as much at home as the new clock Daddy had brought home and hung in the kitchen.

Mother didn't object to the ugly clock. I thought she might. I told her about the clock incident at church, and how after it came down an elder's wife explained that since the clock had been removed, we needed to install a trap door behind the pulpit and hand her the remote control. Mother didn't laugh the way we all knew so well. She would keep a poker face when initially amused, often keeping her gaze down as her brown eyes began to sparkle with merriment. When the laughter would finally erupt, her cheeks flushed pink, her eyes watered, and her shoulders shook. That's how Mother could laugh. But after Uncle Tommy died, she never laughed like that again.

Daddy tried to console Mother during the first hard days after Uncle Tommy's death, but even the usual words of comfort, "He's in a better place now," rang hollow when compared with Mother's wail that I remembered from the funeral: "He's my brother! He's my brother!"

That lament stayed with me as I considered the implications of how three small words could tell so big a story. I watched and listened very carefully to my mother, who seemed to live more and more inside herself.

Mother maintained the same routines as before. She cooked the same meals. She had the same types of conversations. Only it all happened from a distance. A part of Mother disappeared with Uncle Tommy and never came back, but Daddy didn't notice. He was too busy trying to get her attention.

He stalked her around the house, giggling when she got mad and told him to light somewhere. If she sent him outside to find something to do, he hid behind a tree in the front yard and watched Mary Ellen's house and mine to see what we were up to. He checked our mail when he went to get his own to see who was writing us. And he developed one of the worst cases of dandruff we had ever seen. Mother bought all the dandruff shampoos, and then she switched to baby products that were hypoallergenic. She even changed her laundry detergent. But nothing helped. We teased Daddy about it: "You're one big flake!" we told him. He didn't seem to mind. He basked in the attention.

One day when I went over for coffee, he and I were standing by the kitchen windows. He was slurping a rare cup of decaf while I was brushing the snow of white flakes from his shoulders. Suddenly he exclaimed, "Good night, Miss Agnes! There are a lot of dead birds lying out in the back yard. It looks like a Hitchcock movie."

Mother and I both jumped at the news of the catastrophe. I strained to look where Daddy was staring while Mother joined us at the windows. "Those are leaves, Jerry," Mother said darkly. "Why are you always trying to shock us?"

"Yes, Daddy," I said, moving closer to Mother. Adrenaline had made my heart race, and I took a deep breath to slow down my heartbeat. "They're just leaves."

"They're not dead birds?" he asked, surprised.

I shook my head, looking up at him. He wasn't being dramatic or playing a game.

"Your daddy needs a lot of attention," Mother said, taking a deep breath.

"You want to listen to my heart?" Daddy asked, proving her right.

I said yes one more time, and pronounced his heart beating just as it should. "I guess I'm all right, although Patty Kate says that something else is wrong with me."

"Psychologists always think something is wrong with everybody," I replied. Patty had recently earned her master's in psychology and was now a counselor at a local college.

"We're just getting older, aren't we?" Daddy asked.

"Yes," I said. "We are all getting older."

But it was more than that. We were all steadily separating. A big part of Mother had disappeared when her brother did. Daddy wasn't acting like himself. Julie Ann and Big Jody had moved, and were now hours away in Memphis. Patty Kate was trying to build a life for herself and her daughter during the hardest time of her life. Mary Ellen still lived next door to me, but the business with Matthew and the quarters had caused a deep chasm. When I asked a question about what the future might be, there was no one to answer it but me. I missed my parents and my sisters. I wrote stories to keep myself company.

One morning while I was sitting on the sofa, looking out my front picture window, I asked myself this question: What would happen if Mother disappeared completely like Uncle Tommy did?

I picked up my clipboard and began to write a novel that would answer that question. I called it "The Mother Lode." It felt to me like a very serious book, but when other people read it, they chuckled too often. I thought it was a mystery, but other people thought it was a comedy.

I shoved the strange book under the bed next to "The Prayermaker" and wondered what to do next. Day or night, I did my best thinking staring out my picture window. I found myself watching for Mary Ellen, monitoring her coming and going almost as if I were Daddy. One evening, after hearing more traffic than usual on the road, I looked out the window to see a trailer attached to my brother-in-law's car. It was stacked with furniture.

That was the night that Mary Ellen and her family carted off their possessions in the dark without a word and moved to a place they didn't tell us about. It was as if aliens had come and gotten them. I didn't report this news to my parents, who now only rarely asked about Matthew or Mary Ellen. It was a peculiar response to a division in our family that they had created. They lived in denial that they might have been, if not wrong about the missing quarters, then at the very least shortsighted in judging anyone out loud.

Only after new neighbors moved into the house Daddy had built for my sister, assuming ownership of the third mailbox in our trio of family mailboxes, did my parents fully recognize that their oldest daughter had taken her family to a place not next door to them. What did they feel about this? I did not know, for we did not discuss it, just as we did not discuss the fact that Patty Kate and her baby daughter Katie, who had been living with them for the past year, were now ready to move out.

It felt too soon. But Patty had a good job, and she wanted her own home. I agreed in theory, but I didn't want to lose another sister. Mother and I both liked having Patty Kate and Katie with us.

Daddy felt otherwise. Mother said Daddy was jealous of the baby, and that the jealousy was making him do strange things for attention, like putting letters in the mailbox that didn't have stamps on them. This irritated Mother no end. And then came the morning when Mother ran out of her own supply of stamps. Knowing that Daddy hoarded all kinds of supplies in his office, Mother went upstairs to search the big desk for a roll of stamps.

She didn't find any.

Not believing that Daddy would have run out of stamps, she

thrust her hand deeply into the lap drawer of the desk. She found three rolls of new Scotch tape that Daddy kept in reserve, because he claimed one of us was always stealing his tape, and sometimes, the key to his safety-deposit box. She found her own pair of small scissors that had gone missing from the kitchen drawer where she always kept them to open vacuum-packed food. And then her hand bumped into a lumpy felt sack.

I was downstairs waiting for the coffee to finish dripping when my Mother's hand found that missing pouch. The whole house went still for a moment, the way a room that is filled with people can suddenly become silent. I paused in the stillness of my mother's moment of truth being born in her. The power of that knowledge filled her and then pulsed through the house.

Mother had found the missing coins that her grandson had been accused of stealing. When she came down the stairs, her face white with tension, Daddy let loose one of his long, shrill wolf whistles. Time had not changed him. Mother's irritation over the whistling had not stopped his mouth from pursing or the high-pitched sound from blasting forth like a siren announcing an emergency.

I watched Mother not slap his whistling face. Instead, she held out the black pouch of bicentennial quarters that Matthew was supposed to have taken. "Look what I have found," she said.

Daddy read the hidden message instantly, but he didn't waver. "So, the boy brought them back. Who knows how he snuck in here and planted them where one of us would find them? Probably happened when we were at church. It's the only time he knows for sure we won't be here."

"You didn't put them in your own desk drawer and forget that's where they were? Way in the back of the drawer behind my kitchen scissors that you stole and the rolls of Scotch tape that you hoard?"

"Is that where you found them, Mother?" Daddy asked, laughing. His laugh was not joyful, not truly teasing. It was mocking and aggressive. I paused for a moment to consider the nature of that particular laugh. It felt evil to me, and I marveled that I could feel that response to any characteristic of Daddy's nature.

"I wonder why Matthew didn't put them back in the file cabinet where he found them? That would have been more logical. I used to keep them in the desk till I moved them to the safety-deposit box," Daddy said.

"They were in the safety-deposit box?" I asked suddenly, my voice breaking. "You have the key. When did you get them out?"

"Your Mother has a key." He eyed her suspiciously. "But your mother doesn't drive, so it couldn't have been . . ."

I interrupted his train of thought before he got himself into worse trouble.

"Why didn't you just leave them there?" I asked, moving to stand between my parents, for I felt that death was coming our way right across our woods, and I wanted to intercept it if I could. Daddy didn't feel this, didn't know that life was in danger. Not his life, not her life — but the goodness of life. Love's nature was afflicted by his perception, contaminated by his false accusations. "None of this would have happened if you had just left the coins in the safety-deposit box," I declared.

"I couldn't look at them if they were in the safety-deposit box." His voice assumed an unpleasant whine. "I like to look at them."

He took the black felt pouch from Mother and poured a palmful of quarters on the table. Then he began to create level stacks of coins, like a gambler lining up his winnings.

"Matthew didn't steal your coins, and he did not bring them back. They've been there all along," I asserted in a rare posture of defiance.

Daddy dismissed my statement authoritatively with a wave of his hand. "Maybe he did. Maybe he didn't. They're here now. That's all that matters. I'd forgotten how many I have. Let's have some fresh coffee to celebrate."

Mother slumped in a nearby chair. Her face looked tired, and her color wasn't good.

I didn't ask her what they were going to do about repairing the relationship with their oldest daughter and their grandson. I didn't ask her the questions because she and I both knew there weren't any answers. Something was wrong with Daddy, and we didn't know what it was or how to fix it. Instead, I asked her, "Are you getting enough rest?"

Mother didn't answer my question directly. "Your daddy isn't sleeping so good these days."

"What are you saying about me? I heard my name mentioned. It better be something good." Daddy's posture straightened, and he grinned. He looked about expectantly as if a surprise party in his honor might suddenly erupt.

"I'm saying that you are having a hard time putting on your own clothes," Mother said tiredly. She wouldn't look at me, but the knowledge of a personal defeat she had not intended to disclose began to seep out of her and into me.

"We play the baby game, and I'm the baby!" Daddy exclaimed, giggling. It was a strange, high-pitched giggle that made my flesh crawl. He rubbed his hands together gleefully.

Mother explained, her voice low. "He pretends he can't dress himself, and I have to help him do it. He loved it when I got the baby shampoo for his hair. Patty says he's jealous of my attention to Katie. It's another one of the reasons she wants to move out.

"Ever since I started taking care of Katie, he's gotten more and more possessive of me. He follows me everywhere. Everywhere! His temper can be awful short too. You don't see it. He hides it from you, but I don't dare leave him alone with Katie. I tried it just once. Her screaming woke me up fast." Mother leaned toward me and confided, "It'll be better for them to move out." And when she said those secret words I saw that my mother had stories inside of her that belonged only to her. I saw that in a moment, and then her eyes clouded again, and the truth was hidden once more behind the expression she had learned to wear in the dream house.

"What are you two whispering about? About me? I'm telling you — it better be something good!"

"It wouldn't be anything else," I promised him. "Daddy, how are you feeling?"

"I'd feel better if I could get some sleep," he declared, picking up on the last sentence of Mother's explanation. He eyed her accusingly.

"The television is on the blink. Sometimes it comes on in the night by itself."

"Your daddy wakes me up to come down and turn it off. He can't work the remote anymore."

"I've considered the idea that your mama might be trying to drive me crazy with the TV so she can have all my money." He said the words as if they were a joke, but there was a hidden message in them — a message meant for me to hear. I heard it.

"Yeah. All that money," Mother moaned. "I know how much money there is."

And I knew. Daddy announced his net worth each year after he had his income tax figured. The net balance had not increased in three years. I hadn't really thought about what that meant. Daddy had always made money.

"Mother, what do you think is wrong with Daddy?" I asked.

"Ain't nothing wrong with your daddy that killing him wouldn't fix," Mother said loudly. He interpreted that comment as flirting. Mother looked at Daddy as if he were a stranger.

I had seen that particular expression before. It took me a few seconds, but then I remembered when I had seen it. It was the last time her sister Phyllis was in town, the day that the refrigerator stopped working.

From the Family Album . . .

Causes and Effects

No one announced when I entered the kitchen last Saturday night that there was trouble. I found that out for myself. When I opened the freezer door to get some ice for my water glass, my fingertips grazed

the bottom of the ice-maker's bucket, and I felt a good inch of standing water. I closed the freezer door, sat down at the kitchen table, and
acted like I hadn't wanted anything cold to drink after all. I watched
for some sign from my mother that she was aware that the appliance
on her left was not working, but she was preoccupied with counting
pork chops.

"I'm not here to eat," I assured her.

She heard that and looked up, concerned. "You could eat a little
something," she replied automatically.

"No, ma'am. You go ahead and have your dinner."

Mother fixed plates for Aunt Phyllis and Dad. Julie was home for a
visit, too. She was squeezed in next to Patty, who sat quietly beside the
high chair where Katie played with her food. They all drank glasses of
tap water without complaint, eyeing the unusually silent coffeepot.
No one mentioned the lack of ice. It was only after Daddy had gotten
his strength back from his pork chop and some lima beans that he was
able to ask me, "Do you think too many people have been opening the
icebox? Could that be the reason it isn't chilling properly?"

I was not surprised that he couldn't face the news that there
was work to be done. Increasingly, he had become disassociated
from working around the house. Maybe after a lifetime of fixing
whatever was broken, he was just used up. I responded truthfully,
"Oh, I think it's something more, because there's water standing in
the freezer."

Then, in a whisper loud enough to be overheard, Daddy reported
to me that he believed someone had fooled around with the tempera-
ture knob inside. His unspoken question lingered in the air. Logic told
him that before our visiting aunt arrived, the fridge was working
properly; now that she was here, it was broken. Was there a connection? Had Aunt Phyl fiddled with the knob or simply jinxed us by
coming for a visit?

As Daddy struggled to define the problem, Aunt Phyl heard
Daddy's question and considered the implications. After a moment,
she announced solemnly, "I do not touch other people's knobs."

Her brief speech stirred me to say the words no one wanted to hear. "The refrigerator is broken, and it isn't going to fix itself."

It took my saying that aloud before Daddy could face the truth, but there is a proper pacing to solving a problem, and grieving that there is work to be done is a natural first step. Daddy demonstrated that he was finally ready to take on the burden of confronting the problem by asking everyone to leave the room.

Of course, no one left the room except Aunt Phyl, because she doesn't know that we never leave the room when Daddy asks us to. We just get still. Then, while we were pretending to be invisible, Daddy went to the garage and got his portable air compressor and plugged it into the kitchen outlet.

Right away the air compressor blew out a fuse, but no one complained. That cause and effect was understandable. Daddy and I replaced the fuse, which inspired confidence, for it proved to us once again that we could diagnose trouble and correct it.

The power back on, I switched Daddy's plug to another outlet, while he removed the grill from the front of the fridge.

When I saw what he was up to, I rose and got the vacuum cleaner. We worked without talking. While Daddy aimed the air compressor's nozzle and blew all kinds of stuff out from under the icebox, I vacuumed up the flying debris. As I worked, I did wonder how what we were doing could fix the refrigerator.

Reading my mind, Daddy explained, "I saw someone else blow dirt out from under his broken refrigerator once, and it fixed his icebox."

Mother spoke up. "Your Daddy would have blown it out earlier today, but the vacuum cleaner bag needed replacing." Sometimes Mother can explain Daddy's behavior when he cannot explain himself. This was one of those occasions. Daddy was having trouble doing small jobs like changing the vacuum cleaner's bag. I knew that he was almost terrified of a broken refrigerator. Where his reason failed him, being afraid began to take hold.

"Don't worry. I can change the bag," I promised. Swiftly I flipped the lid and removed the overfull bag. I installed a new bag with the ease of a gas-pump jockey changing a flat tire.

When it was obvious that I was finished, Daddy knelt down beside me and said, "Let me help you."

"Thanks, but she's already done," I said, slapping the hood back on the belly of the cleaner.

"Good night, Miss Agnes! You're fast!" he said, but what he meant was, "I'm sorry."

"How's the icebox? Any cool air blowing yet?" I asked, shrugging off his praise.

Before he could answer, Mother interrupted excitedly. "Look! Here's my missing domino. I've looked all over the kitchen for this double-six. I haven't been able to play dominoes in weeks."

We had all been witness to the evaporation of this dotted bone, and though a half-dozen of us had scoured this room on hands and knees, we had not been able to make that treasured domino reappear. The loss of it had been confusing. We had been unable to understand why something so undeniably concrete that had just been present among us could so fluidly slip away.

Weeks ago when she lost her favored game piece, Mother did not go out and buy a new domino set. She had trusted that the missing piece would reappear in time.

It was that moment when the domino reappeared that I knew the refrigerator was fixed. Though I couldn't explain how blowing dirt from under the icebox would have anything to do with making it chill again, I knew that the weekend had been saved and that my aunt's reputation as a jinx would be minimized. For, as I assembled the equation in my mind, although trouble had arrived with her, it did not stay.

Mother hurriedly stashed that lucky game piece in her special wooden box, and Daddy went to put away the air compressor. On his way to his work shed, he issued instructions in the same bold way he had once spoken as a preacher who promised an ultimate arrival at the promised land: "Now, if you will all keep your hands off that icebox door and give the water a chance to freeze, we'll have ice again sooner rather than later."

The room came to life as order took the place of chaos. Aunt Phyl rejoined the circle of our family clan at the dinner table, which had been cleared. Mother finally plugged in the coffeepot, and once he had a cup in front of him, Daddy told the story of when he was a little boy living in Florida. Some older men who lived next door dared him to pull a dead alligator out of a pond with a long-handled rake. "Only the alligator just looked dead! The second I slipped that noose around his neck, he came to life quick enough," Daddy recalled, his voice becoming once again that of a child.

I asked Daddy if the men who had given him the rake and asked him to pull out the alligator had promised him a reward for retrieving the carcass or a share of the profits from the sale of the alligator skin. He confessed to me that he had not thought that far ahead when he was offered the adventure of pulling a dead alligator from its watery bed. He said that he had done it for the reward of seeing an alligator up close.

"What did you do when you realized you had a-hold of a live alligator?" Aunt Phyl asked.

"What would you have done?" he replied with a question.

She didn't answer, and no one else tried. Words would have been redundant, as they so often are when a question arises that requires action for its solution. Given time to think, everyone in the room knew the right response to holding a rake attached to a live alligator.

9

The Sleeping Alligator

Daddy finally admitted that something besides his heart problem was wrong with him, only he didn't want to say what exactly because it had to do with his personal parts. After much shuffling and evasive answering, he finally admitted that his penis had a bend in it, and he couldn't get it straightened out.

Covering her mouth with a hand so she wouldn't laugh out loud or scream (I couldn't tell which), Mother left the room, ostensibly to go be with her granddaughter Katie. Patty's daughter was in the back room watching *Mary Poppins* on the Disney Channel.

After Daddy apologized for saying the word *penis* out loud to me, a single woman and his daughter, I assured him that I had heard of penises and that it was all right because I had known for some time that he had one. Now that he had identified the source of his problem, we'd find a solution, I promised.

Then he said he had counted on my saying that and had made an appointment with a doctor, but he was afraid to drive the car in his condition. I didn't see how a bend in any portion of his anatomy might cause him to have car trouble, but I assured him that I'd be happy to take him. I went back to my house and got dressed, putting on the same outfit I wear to see any other doctor: jeans and a top. I carefully drew on a balanced pair of resolute eyebrows. The drawn expression did not in any way imply alarm.

I did wonder how a bent penis could produce the weird behaviors

Daddy had been manifesting. Did it have any connection to the baby game he played with Mother? Could a broken penis make a man para- noid about being stolen from? I theorized that it could worry him enough to cause sleeplessness and that chronic insomnia might pro- duce confused thinking. If we could get his problem solved, his anxi- ety might be relieved, and he could sleep better, and Mother could sleep, and they wouldn't be cross with each other anymore, and we could all live happily ever after. Then I could call Mary Ellen on the telephone and explain how life with Daddy had gotten all bent out of shape, and couldn't she understand? Maybe after all this time, she would even laugh with me again.

An hour later, I was sitting in a roomful of men who wouldn't look me in the eye. They were all staring at their zippers and groan- ing. The doctor summoned Daddy to the back room, and I was left alone with the mournful men who would not look up. Fifteen min- utes later, I was beckoned to the back room, where the doctor told me that there was nothing that could be done about Daddy's condition — that this happens to some men as they age — and it shouldn't inter- fere with marital relations, and did I need to hear the whole explana- tion again? And I said, "No. Thanks a whole lot."

In the car on the way home, Daddy pretended that I was Mother, and he began to create a story about how exuberant passion must have been the cause of his problem. He suddenly felt free to discuss the potential of his anatomy with great frankness. I listened, praying that he would soon change the subject, and just when I was about to give up hope, he finally did.

As we were about to take the access ramp to the interstate that crosses the Alabama River, Daddy stopped being a nervous but re- deemed lover and again became, inexplicably and undeniably, the man I knew as my father. With no warning at all, he then told me an- other story.

"Before I knew your mother — before I joined the service and went off for a year — I knew a girl. She was a nice girl — a little fast — and I left her alone to go in the service. There wasn't time to get married." He said the words nervously.

I saw his jaw muscle work, and he declared forthrightly, as if making a confession to a priest, "I should have taken the time to make an honest woman of her, though I didn't really want to marry her. This happened before I got saved. This girl might have been pregnant. I think she must have done something to get rid of the baby — if there really was a baby. I don't know for sure. By the time I got back home, the girl was gone for good. She got married to someone else, and the last I heard she had a house full of children."

"Oh, Daddy," I sighed.

He stopped me from expressing sympathy or asking any questions by pressing onward with his story, which needed to be told. The truth is like that. It can abide untold for years, but once it starts to break through, there's no stopping it.

"I'm telling you this because. . . ." He stumbled momentarily.

I didn't interrupt him. I waited till he found his words.

"Do you think I'm having problems with my p-p-personal parts because I let that girl down? I mean, justice has a way of catching up with you."

I shook my head. "What you're suggesting is not justice. And I don't think the relationship you had with that girl before you knew Jesus or Mother has anything to do with the present affliction of your personal parts."

"You don't think it could?" he asked me seriously. "Because the Bible says, 'As ye sow, so shall ye reap.'"

"Yes. The Bible says that, but there's a delicate blend of timing and judgment that must occur when applying the truths of the Bible to one's life. Logic doesn't always work. The Holy Spirit helps us to do that."

"I've never really been sure how justice and grace fit together. We're not off the hook just because we're saved. There are consequences to be paid for what we do this side of the grave," he said solemnly. "And that's only fair."

"That's right," I agreed. "But God also says that his wisdom is far above ours, and we can't really understand the full nature of his justice and how he applies it in mercy. God allows for us to be confused. We call those times living in faith."

As if he hadn't heard me, Daddy mused, "There are consequences, but we can't always know for sure if what we're experiencing now is a consequence of something we did before. . . ."

"Or if there is any guilt involved," I theorized softly, "since we live a forgiven life. The Bible also says that certain kinds of trouble are appointed so that the Lord can be glorified."

"I don't think this is one of those occasions," he admitted. His mouth was beginning to work into a smile.

"No," I said. "I don't see how this particular trouble can be one of those times. Is there anything else that's worrying you? You can tell me."

He stared out at the Alabama River. The afternoon light filtering through the clouds cast a silver sheen upon the timeless water, more beautiful than people have a right to expect from just an ordinary phenomenon that we dismiss by the casual name *daylight*. When was the last time I had stopped to send God a report that I was aware of the magnanimousness of his nature that overflowed daily in the direction of my family and me? Before I could follow this interior trail of repentance, Daddy continued his truth-telling. His voice contained a humility that pierced my heart.

"At night I hear people downstairs playing dominoes. But when I go downstairs, no one is there."

"I hear bumps in the night too. I think that's pretty normal. You don't think the TV is coming on by itself anymore?"

"Sometimes it does. Or it seems to. Maybe your mother comes to bed and forgets to turn off the TV. She comes to bed later and later now. I don't know when she sleeps. Then I wake up and go downstairs, and maybe the TV hasn't come on by itself. Maybe it was just never turned off."

"That sounds perfectly reasonable to me, Daddy."

He took a deep breath, for the truth was still pouring from him, and he couldn't stop now. "I can't make the remote control work. I struggle and struggle, but I can't turn it off. My fingers are too big for the buttons."

"Have you checked the batteries?" I asked.

He looked at me, perplexed. "No. We never check the batteries in the remote. I forgot it had batteries."

"When the batteries start to go bad, you can point that remote at the TV forever, and it won't do a thing. You have to open the little backside and roll the batteries around with your thumb till they make a better connection, but that only works for a little while. Eventually, in order to keep from throwing the remote control against the wall or killing yourself, you have to put in new batteries."

"I can't believe I never thought of that. That may be all there is to it. You're something else, you know that? I don't know who you take after."

"I take after you. And Mother."

"You're too smart to take after me. I know you're smart. If I had had any book learning, maybe I could have made something of myself."

"I've had book learning, and I haven't accomplished as much as you have."

"You're everything a father could want in a daughter . . . and a friend."

Just then the clouds parted, and the sunlight fell like a banquet of light. Daddy and I saw it at the same time, covering the river water with more than filtered rays — it was bright enough to be called holy. *I felt the presence of Love.* It was beautiful, and Daddy and I smiled at one another because we could share it.

We rode the rest of the way home in love and in the companionable silence of people who find each other agreeable. When we reached home, Daddy flung back the front door excitedly and hurried inside as if he were about to proclaim a miraculous healing. Mother was working her crossword puzzle and did not look up.

"The doctor said there's nothing to worry about. It won't interfere with, uh-hmm, marital relations."

Mother replied, her voice rich with irony, "I was really worried about that." Looking at me, she asked quietly, "Did you have a good time?"

"I'd like to do that again real soon," I said, plopping down onto the small, barrel-shaped chair that could spin around. The grandchildren liked it. I began to spin myself around in circles because the action fit my mood. When I came to a stop, I said, "The sign on the doctor's door said that he was a urologist."

"That's what some penis doctors call themselves so that men can come and go without people staring at their zippers," Mother said.

"You know about that, do you?"

"My brothers explained it to me from time to time," she replied. "Thanks for carting the old man around."

"You bet," I said, rising. I thought my parents needed to be alone.

"Are you in a hurry?" Daddy asked, suddenly aware of me as someone who was grown and worked for a living. He hadn't thought of that all day.

"No. I'm not in a particular hurry, but I do have work to do."

"Have I caused you to be late with one of your columns?" His eyes flooded, and he licked his lips, getting ready to apologize. I stopped him.

"No, sir. I stay a few columns ahead. It would take more than a morning at the personal parts doctor to throw me off my schedule."

"That's good. You always were a smart worker. Thanks, Buddy," he whispered as I threw my arms around him and squeezed him tightly until he started to laugh. He never minded my loving him full out or the hugs that proclaimed my enthusiasm for him.

"I'll be missing you till I see you again," he said, following me to the doorway.

"I live right there," I said, pointing to my yellow house down the road. "You can come and visit me if you get desperate to see my face."

"Don't make fun of my love," he said, and he wasn't joking this time.

"I never underestimate the gift of your love," I replied. "I love you too."

He nodded soberly. Then he cast a glance at himself in the pink-tinted mirror and smiled at his reflection. He was feeling better. Mother was trying not to laugh. It was a good way to leave them. I ambled down the road with only a wave behind me. We had stopped saying good-bye years ago.

Once I was inside my own house, I made three phone calls. I called Julie Ann first, who listened closely but quietly as I described Daddy's problem. Taking a deep breath, I called Mary Ellen next, wondering if she would pick up. She didn't like to talk on the phone. She too received the news silently, but I figured that she wasn't over being hurt with Daddy. I called Patty last. She listened like a trained counselor and then commented, "Maybe the cruise to the Bahamas that you planned for them will help them both feel better."

I had almost forgotten about the cruise.

Could Daddy go on a romantic cruise in his condition without having a nervous breakdown from insecurity or embarrassment?

Could Mother go on a romantic cruise without laughing?

Hoping to feel relieved by sharing the news of what could be causing Daddy's odd behaviors, I was jarred by the mention of the cruise. I began to have a strange sense of foreboding that my parents were not going on a second honeymoon but were about to embark on a dangerous journey and that, without meaning to, I had put their lives in jeopardy.

From the Family Album . . .

Sweet Dreams of a Cruise

It was pouring down rain the morning I was scheduled to drive my folks to the airport. They were catching a plane in order to catch a boat — their first, long-dreamed-about cruise. Daylight Savings Time had just kicked in, so it was still dark.

My dressing time was brief. I drew on a pair of Bon Voyage eyebrows, pulled on a weatherproof parka over my clothes, grabbed an umbrella, and headed down the road to my parents' house, where no light shone to indicate that they were even awake. I knocked aggressively, determined that they were not going to miss their plane.

Daddy answered the door, his face drawn. Behind him, a single lightbulb burned softly. "We hate like the devil to drag you out on a morning like this," he apologized, as if there was an emergency happening and not just the beginning of a vacation.

"I love to be up this time of day," I said, waving gaily at the moon over my shoulder. "It makes me feel as if I'm getting a head start on the day. Are you ready for adventure on the high seas?" My tone was jolly, too forced. I determined to fix it before he noticed that I was scared of sending him and Mother off into the world without a protector — that is, me.

He reached for the aspirin bottle in response. Mother accepted a dose too, and together they sipped Coca-Cola. They moved about forlornly, as if they were two grammar-schoolers headed to the first day of school.

"I'll take care of everything while you're gone," I assured them one more time. "Nothing will change here. Home will be right here when you get back."

They would be gone four days, which was three days longer than any trip they took by car. They had a hard time staying away from the house. But I was not the one sending them on this trip. They were sending themselves. It was a lifelong dream, and they intended to fulfill it. They said they wanted to go, asked me to arrange it; but once I paid the deposit, the cruise stopped being a dream and became a burden. They began to blame me for banishing them from the familiar. They were not on the boat yet, but they were already homesick.

"Our room will have a bathroom, won't it?" Mother asked again.

"Oh, yes. And you should have a window."

"A porthole," Daddy corrected me. His eyes sparkled for an instant, but faded quickly.

"You're wearing your new shirt," I observed, though I also noticed that he was not wearing his new navy skipper's cap. He was wearing an old baseball cap with the words "Coronado Beach Club" on the crown. He did not belong to that club. I had bought the cap for him a year ago on a visit to San Diego, where he had been stationed during his stint in the army. He was wearing it for sentimental reasons. And for courage. Perhaps it made him feel like a soldier, but this wasn't war: it was vacation.

Taking a deep breath, I asked, "Are you ready, Mother?"

"I don't know if I am going to be able to breathe in this brassiere. My chest feels awful tight. I get nervous when I'm going away from home. I think I'm forgetting something I might need."

"Go braless," I advised boldly. "What difference would it make? You'll never see most of those people again."

She ignored me, heading to the bathroom for one last pit stop.

"I better load up the car," Daddy announced, as I grabbed the bigger suitcase and headed out the front door. "Don't you do that," he called after me. "You'll throw your back out."

By the time he finished issuing his warning, I had the trunk door unlocked and his bag installed. Two more awaited me. While Dad fidgeted with an uncooperative umbrella, I loaded the rest of their gear. "I should be doing that," he said.

"As long as one of us can do it, we're all right," I said with a quick grin. I looked up to see if he recalled the time years ago when he had said that very thing to me, the morning he had rescued me when I had a flat tire. He didn't remember at all, and that made me sad.

Car doors closed. Seat belts fastened. Mother lit a cigarette while Daddy shifted in the back seat from left to right to see if he was blocking my view in the mirror. "Your head's okay," I reassured him, nosing the car through the dark and the rain toward an airplane that must first land in Atlanta.

"Are you sure we'll be able to find the other plane we have to catch?" Mother asked.

"There will be a person waiting just as you exit the first plane who'll tell you where to go. You'll be fine."

I wasn't sure if I was telling them the truth. I had just had a hard time getting them in the car. I did not know if they could negotiate the Atlanta airport.

"We didn't eat breakfast," Daddy announced suddenly. "They're going to feed us, aren't they? Your mother made me drink a Coke, and now I'm sick to my stomach."

"They'll give you something to eat on the next flight. On this first one — the shuttle — you can get some milk or coffee."

"I think I'll take the milk. Should I tell the lady as soon as I get on the plane?"

"An attendant will come by to check your seat belt. Tell her or him what you want," I advised.

"What are you going to do today?" Mother asked me, forcing her voice to be a bright imitation of mine.

Before I could answer, Daddy said, "Promise me you'll just go home and not leave the house the rest of the day. This kind of weather is tailor-made for accidents."

"I don't really have anything to do that will make me go out again," I said. I wasn't promising anything, but it sounded like it.

"I bet you're going to go home and make a whole pot of coffee and watch *Bewitched*," Mother predicted. Her tone changed from forced perkiness to forlorn wistfulness. I had not watched *Bewitched* in years. She was speaking for herself.

I recalled what the travel agent had told me, and I repeated it to them: "Sharon says that if you don't have a good time, it's because you've stayed in your room and watched movies the whole trip."

"You mean there's TV onboard?" Mother asked, incredulous.

"Once we go on this cruise, we don't ever have to take another one," Daddy announced suddenly, solemnly.

"Why did you want to go on this one? You sound like you're being tortured!" I snapped.

"Your mother and I aren't getting any younger," Daddy explained. "And we have always dreamed of going on a cruise. We decided now was the time to do it or else."

"Or else you'd be home watching *Bewitched* and drinking coffee?"

"Not me. I'm going to have a glass of milk. Your mother made me drink a Coke, and it has upset my stomach."

At the airport I looked around for a machine that sold milk, but there wasn't one. I was afraid that the first short flight might not have

milk. I pushed this concern away by helping my folks redo their lug-
gage tags, which they had done wrong. The ticket processor helped,
his eyes never meeting mine.

I guided my parents to the flight gate. Daddy and I sat down to
wait for the boarding call. Mother headed to the smoking lounge. Nervously, she lit one cigarette after another, attempting to build up her
nicotine level before getting on a non-smoking flight.

Daddy fretted that Mother was taking too long, and he asked me if
he should fetch her. "We can see her from here," I soothed him. "Look!
She's all right."

Mother returned and smiled brightly. I smiled a reflected version
of this false cheer. Then the attendant called for the first boarders, and
I escorted my parents to the plane. Finally, boarding passes in hand,
my parents filed away like children on a fire drill.

I walked away and did not look back. At home, I called Julie Ann
to tell her that our parents were on their way to the Bahamas.

Julie groaned. "I can't stand it. Do you think they'll be all right?"

"Someone is supposed to tell them where to go and what to do the
whole time. How could they get lost?" I repeated what the travel
agent had said about reasons people didn't have a good time on a
cruise.

Four days later my parents returned. They were late. They had
missed their connecting flight, but Delta had put them on the next
one. We drove home in silence, but as soon as we were back where we
all belonged, they explained how they had missed the plane. They had
split up to go to the bathroom in the Atlanta airport and had gotten
lost coming out of their respective restrooms.

"That lady didn't give us good directions, or else we didn't hear them
very well. Your mother got kind of upset. She started to cry, but I bought
her a Sara Lee coffee roll and a carton of milk, and she got all right."

"I told him to call you to come and get us. It's not like Atlanta is in
the middle of nowhere," Mother said.

"I'd have been right there," I promised her.

I asked about the food on the ship.

"They had anything you could want to eat," Daddy marveled. "You could order anything on the menu, and double portions if you were that hungry. I ordered double strawberry shortcake."

Mother interrupted. "The meat was tender. I had a piece of tenderloin that was this high. It looked small, but by the time I cut it up and chewed piece after piece, it seemed much bigger. And we gambled. Your daddy won twenty-five, maybe thirty dollars on the slot machines with one quarter."

"We watched other people play blackjack. You ought to see how fast those dealers' hands move. Shoot, they were so fast that they actually changed dealers, and we didn't see it happen," Daddy said.

"That is fast," I agreed. "What did you think of the barbecue on the island and the prices on the in-port shopping?"

"We never got off the ship," Mother said, looking away. She didn't want to talk about that.

"They had some small boats that went back and forth to shore, but we didn't want to risk getting lost or sunburned. We watched the people coming back. They looked ruined," Daddy said.

"You never got off the boat?" I asked, disbelieving.

"Wasn't any need to. They had anything you could possibly want right there on the ship," Daddy explained.

"Every time we left the cabin, a steward came in and emptied the trash can and put out fresh ice," Mother elaborated. "You could pick up the phone day or night and order a pot of coffee. Before you had the phone down good, the man was there knocking on the door, and you never had to tip him. After dinner you'd go back to your room and there'd be a chocolate mint on the pillow and a card that read *Sweet Dreams*. That was some of the best chocolate I have ever put in my mouth."

"And the movies on the TV were all new — the kind you usually have to pay real money to see. Every time I turned on the set, I saw Al Pacino. You know that movie where he played the blind man?" Daddy asked.

"How was it?"

"Couldn't tell you," he said. "I never saw the whole movie all the way through. We had a window in our room. It was big, like a picture window. You could almost reach out and touch the water. In the Baha-mas, the water is real blue."

For a second, I envisioned the Bahamas. The blue water. The dif-ferent possible adventures. The romantic descriptions in the brochure the travel agent sent over when my parents began to consider the trip.

"The weak part of the trip was coming back home. That's when we weren't sure what we were doing," Daddy said.

"It wore us out," Mother explained. "We had to find our own bags. We put them on one bus, and then we got on another bus. We were never sure that our bags were headed home."

"Then we missed the plane. Your mother got upset until I bought her a Sara Lee coffee roll and a carton of milk." Daddy leaned over and whispered, "She was getting ready to cry."

"I would have come and gotten you," I vowed one more time. "It's just a two-hour drive." (It's three hours, and I don't know why I lied.)

"No need to," Daddy said. "The airline put us on the next plane. We wouldn't have gotten held up if the lady had given us good direc-tions. Or maybe we didn't hear her right."

"Did your stomach straighten out?" I asked.

"It never got real bad, but it never got better, either. There was a cafeteria on that ship where you could eat all you wanted night and day. I went there the last day and got two take-out breakfasts, but your mother couldn't eat any, so I ate them both."

Daddy excused himself, and when he did, Mother said, "Your daddy wandered around in the airport for twenty minutes, and I couldn't find him and he couldn't find me. That's why I was about to cry. His sense of direction isn't what it used to be. We didn't get off the ship because we weren't sure we could find our way back on."

"That's okay. You enjoyed yourself, didn't you?"

She wouldn't look at me directly. "Every time we left the room, someone came in and emptied the trash and put out fresh ice. At night there was a piece of candy on the pillow and a card that read *Sweet Dreams*. It was funny having someone do that."

III

WILDERNESS

10

A Disappearing Act

I have often relied upon the ability to become invisible; and like my mother, who is an expert at tuning out a man who whistles at her and stalks her, I can pretty much will myself into nonentity whenever I wish. Although I learned this technique from my mother, she and I exercise it in different times and places.

Mother is always visible at family gatherings; sometimes I'm invisible.

In the tradition of church ladies who are neither heard nor seen, Mother is mostly invisible at the church she and Daddy attend. I talk in my church and sometimes pray out loud, and when I do, people see and hear me. I never told my mother about these occasions, for her advice to me when I was growing up in the church was, "Don't volunteer. It sets a dangerous precedent."

Her perspective was practical, based upon survival techniques she had learned as the wife of a man who preached when he was asked and sometimes when he wasn't. If a woman who works at home is seen as available for busy work, people in the church will give her busy work to do. It's better not to open that door. Keep it closed: Don't volunteer.

That advice did not keep Mother from helping me after I volunteered to cater macaroni and cheese for the mission conference at my church one March. I watched while she boiled the pasta, grated the cheese, and made two big pans of it for me to take. It was thick and bubbly, rich with two kinds of cheese. She used two of her special tin-foil pans that she usually reserved for cooking turkeys and ham. When I loaded them up in the car, Mother said in the very same tone she used to tell me never to volunteer, "Men love this dish. Don't tell anyone you didn't cook it." And then she said something that sounded like she was contradicting herself: "Next time, tell them you'll bring cherry cobbler."

I did not see that suggestion as being contrary to the advice "Never volunteer." Rather, it was emblematic of her understanding that life was a series of ideals and compromises. This tension boiled down to "Don't volunteer, but if you do, make sure your contribution is the best it can be."

I liked that about my mother, though I was not able to tell her. I did begin to write a column about her, however, and while I was writing it, the phone rang.

"Are you busy?" Mother asked.

I felt like I was the busiest person I knew, although I didn't leave the house very often. I had also been trained to always deny that I was ever really busy, as a show of politeness. Whoever called and asked that question was supposed to hear the answer, "No, not at all." But on this particular day, I told Mother the truth: "I'm writing a column about how much I liked that movie *Dodsworth,* and how, when you saw it, you didn't like it as much."

The phone went silent. I thought Mother was trying to recall the movie, so I offered her memory a nudge. "Don't you remember the last line Walter Huston says — 'Love's got to stop someplace short of suicide'? That's a priceless line."

When she didn't answer me, I grew irritable. "You have to agree that it's a good line," I asserted.

Mother took a deep breath and said, "Phyl is here, and I'm having a domino game tonight." Her voice sounded funny. People must be listening to her end of the conversation. I repented of my irritation.

"Do you want me to come and get Katie?" I whispered.

"If you want to," she said. Her voice seemed distant, and I was tempted to think about what that could mean, but my mind had gone over to the storage cabinet where the videos were stored. Did I own *Dodsworth?* Suddenly I wanted to see it again.

"I'll be right over," I said.

When I got to the dream house, there was a strange rhythm going on inside. Daddy and Uncle Bob, Aunt Phyl's husband, were gone, and Katie wasn't ready for me. She was sitting in her portable swing waving while Mother stood over the old oak dining table, working the daily Jumble while she timed herself on the kitchen clock. I scooped up Katie, grabbed the travel kit that Patty kept stocked, and then I stood at the back door, waiting for Mother to feel my attention.

She was oblivious to me. She wore her cut-off jeans, faded from being washed in Clorox, and her hair was already washed and set in yellow plastic rollers. Her mind was pushing letters around while she was halfway-listening to Aunt Phyl; she had already dismissed me. I noticed that the house was uncharacteristically quiet. Not a single appliance was running: not the dishwasher, not the washing machine, not the clothes dryer. I saw the light from the TV flickering, but the sound was muted, and I wondered why they didn't just turn it off. The TV was on all the time now, whether anyone was in the living room or not.

"Where's Daddy?" I asked.

"Doctor," Aunt Phyl said succinctly. She met my gaze. "Bob took him," she added, and then she smiled as if to reassure me that Daddy was all right — don't worry. I nodded and waited for Mother to add a word of good-bye, but she was engrossed in the Jumble. Aunt Phyl smiled indulgently and mouthed the words, "Your mother loves her puzzles."

Something held me in that moment of time, and I repeated my good-bye to Mother twice: "We're gone. We're gone." But she had tuned me out, and she never looked up at me or the baby again. If I didn't know better, I'd think she had a hearing problem. I closed the door and said to three-year-old Katie, "Nothing is ever going to be the same again."

Just before coffeetime later that afternoon, Aunt Phyl called to report that Mother could not get her breath and that Daddy and Bob were still at the neurologist and Mother appeared to be having a heart attack, and did I think she should dial 911? I answered, controlled but intense, "Yes. Do that."

Aunt Phyl seemed to think that I should call them, but I knew that the paramedics' monitor would post the address and that their response would be speedier if someone at the house where the sick person was called for help.

And then, in slow motion, I shifted into the tempo of eternal time, where Mother already was. Setting aside *Time* magazine, I wondered where my long pants were, because it occurred to me that I couldn't go to the hospital in shorts. I phoned Patty Kate and told her that our Mama was sick and to come fast, and later she would tell me in a surprised tone that I didn't sound like myself.

I scooped up Katie and drove the quarter-mile back down to the dream house, but it was too late to stop Mother from doing what she needed to do: permanently disappear with all of the tact of a quiet church lady who didn't volunteer. She had just been waiting on the right time, when her sister rather than any of her daughters would have to handle the pressure of her rapid departure and live with the memories and the questions.

I experienced several reactions to that moment of my mother's disappearance. Seeing her stretched out on the living-room floor in the posture of taking an escapist nap, I felt the same way I did when I looked at *The Death of Marat,* a painting by Jacques-Louis David. I cataloged the idea: Life does imitate art.

I had not considered the legitimacy of art as a medium of expression and knowing in a long time. I recalled that *The Death of Marat* had a great deal of dark, empty space in the upper half, which contrasted with the subject in the lower half: a naked man stabbed with a stiletto by a mysterious assassin. Using so much dark space as a tool for magnifying the subject had always fascinated me, and the implications were enormous. The killer was represented by the vast darkness of the background.

While we waited for the paramedics, I was thinking these thoughts but also realizing that at a time like this, I was supposed to pray over my mama. So, holding Katie on my hip, I began to petition God to give Mother back to us. I was fervent in that plea but not panicked. I asked in love, and the whole time I was praying, my niece was listening very carefully, and so I didn't say everything. She was too young to hear everything that an adult knows about how people choose between life and death.

She didn't need to know this: While I was praying, I felt a great relief that Mother's travail was over. I didn't even know that I had been so burdened for her until I felt that relief, but she looked so peaceful stretched out on the floor, like she was finally getting some sleep. Her arm was outstretched the way it was when she held a sleeping baby, and I wanted to stop praying and say, "Sssssh, Mama is finally getting some rest." But Katie was with me, and Aunt Phyl was pacing, holding her hand against her mouth to stifle a scream that wasn't too far from the surface, and so my prayer for Mother, headed to God, was spoken with Katie and Aunt Phyl mostly in mind.

At the end, I added something especially for Katie: "Lord, suit yourself." I said it because it's important for a child to know that God is in charge, and he often does things that we don't understand, just like the people who take care of us do, and our responsibility is to adjust to what we cannot always understand or change. So I prayed that last sentence for Katie, who didn't need to know what I knew. I added that line as if she were a future lawyer who might review the verbal contract I was making with God.

When I uttered Katie's prayer clause, I did look up at the ceiling of the room, where my mother's spirit was poised in the corner, waiting for the Angel of Death to escort her to where her own mama and daddy and brothers, Sammy and Tommy, waited to receive her. And I, duplicitous woman, while I was praying for Katie's and Aunt Phyl's sakes, "Heal her, heal her now, Lord," was whispering to my mother, "Go on, Mama. I understand."

I always knew that my mother's disappearance was a timely exit. She was used up and tired of pretending otherwise. She was exhausted from playing the baby game with Daddy.

When my mother died of natural causes, I knew that it wasn't only a heart attack that had killed her. Whatever was wrong with Daddy had simply killed Mama first.

From the Family Album . . .

Say Good-bye

Before the paramedics rushed in with their electric paddles and wicked needles, before they stripped off Mama's shirt and bra and pounded upon her pale, spiritless body, I knew what it would take doctors and hospital administrators an hour to declare: "She is gone."

Shock gave way to first grief, which hit hard, like syringes being plunged into my chest. In the beginning, cakes, pies, casseroles, cards, visits, and phone calls distracted me from the knowledge that my mother had disappeared for good. But after ten days the river of sympathetic wishes and offerings dwindled to a trickle, concluding finally with a dozen of Nancy Anderson's cheese biscuits. Then the polite questions began: How are you? How is your daddy? How are you doing with the baby?

How am I doing? In addition to inheriting my father, who after forty-four years of marriage has few practical skills for widowerhood, I have assumed the responsibility of keeping my niece Katie while my sister Patty works. Before Mother died, she handled the morning shift; I took afternoons. Now I keep Katie all day.

The difference? I, the afternoon playmate, am now the daylong authority figure. I must envision the scope of Katie's needs for the day — and the days to come. Peculiarly, there is a marked difference between the way I view the expectations I have of myself and the way others see me and this challenge. Inherent in expressions of condolence I also hear: *This may be your only chance to know what it's like to be a mother.*

But I'm an aunt, not a mother. I do not need to manufacture a lie in order to make my daily life livable any more than I need a pink-tinted mirror to make me look rosier.

One friend said, "Years ago, God asked me to do something I didn't want to do, and I refused. I have regretted it ever since."

I don't need God-sized guilt to coerce me into keeping a child I love.

At times I feel dared to prove my devotion to my Mother's memory by sacrificing myself for my niece. But I am not afraid to give my life and my time to this child. I relish her company. The sacrifice needed from me is not to keep her but to let her go. To promote her independence.

Like many women who must make a choice about where and how a child spends the parts of every day, I decide to ignore the implicit expectations from strangers about how I am to nurture this child. But I do seek seasoned advice.

Outside church one Sunday morning, I ambush Rachael Jones, a veteran first-grade teacher and mother of three. Rachael knows children. Her two oldest children hurry eagerly inside the sanctuary to find their own way to Sunday school. Margaret, the two-year-old, is fastened to Rachael's hip. I recap my situation.

"Follow me," Rachael says as we enter the building. Like a first-grader, I pad behind the mother-teacher, treading the worn, carpeted path to the children's playroom. I think Rachael is going to point out the room where Katie will be if she comes to church with me. I am wrong.

Instead, Rachael invites me to witness the sacrifice of a mother's love called letting go. Rachael hands Margaret over to the nursery manager, and the child immediately begins crying, "Mama! Mama!"

I know what that scream means: "Don't leave me, Mama!" I stifle that same cry in myself now when the remembered visions arise of my mama lying prone on the brown carpet of her living-room floor, her left arm outstretched, her cheek pillowed against the fleshy upper arm where all of the children in the family had nestled. My mother died in the familiar position she assumed when she stretched out beside Katie when it was naptime. When I think of my mother in death, I try to remember the essence of a mother's pose — her outstretched arm protecting a baby. In death, it became the position of letting us go.

Rachael's voice is firm. She consoles Margaret, but she also preaches to herself and to me. "You have to let them go. It's best for them and for you. But be prepared. You never get used to it. Know the pain and expect it. It's up to you to learn how to live with it."

I nod wordlessly, my jaw clenching. We turn our backs on Margaret and march soldier-like, mother-like, away from her and toward our own Sunday school classrooms. My chest aches with a heaviness that is growing familiar. I am tired with the fatigue of child care, father care, family care.

When the bell signals the beginning of Sunday school, Rachael and I part. I stand in the doorway of The Seekers' classroom, trying to get my bearings. The room is the same. The leader, Rex Snider, is writing names on the prayer board. Mine is there, but Daddy's is gone. Jennie Polk looks up and nods. Her husband Bill is flipping pages in his Bible, getting ready for the lesson. Lori Tennimon is copying the names off the prayer board while her husband Dan is whispering in her ear. She laughs, but when she sees me, she stops suddenly, as if laughing is wrong. Sue Luckey turns to chat with Jennie, and Betty Snider catches my eye and pats the chair next to her.

I hesitate while the others look uncomfortable for a moment, and I wonder if I'm supposed to acknowledge the condolence cards I have read but have not responded to. Doug White slips past me, almost apologetically, and I want to say, "Thank you for the card," but my mouth just won't do that. Suddenly they all nod gently in my direction — almost in unison, really — as if saying "amen" to a prayer, though no one has prayed yet. What they mean is for me to come on inside and be with them.

I love them.

I hold on to that realization while I take a seat next to Betty, who remarks that I look calmer than I did a week ago. It is one of the conversational gambits that feels in this dislocated state called grief both soothing and simultaneously critical. Then she asks, leaning closer, "How are you?"

"I am apprehensive about the future," I confide softly.

She whispers, choosing her words carefully, "That's natural. It's the way life is. Your mother is gone. Nothing is the same. I lost my mother years ago. I still miss her."

We grow quiet as the class comes to order, and I can hear clearly down the hallway. Silence fills the moment. Margaret is no longer crying "Mama!" I do feel calmer. No terrifying scenes of the past or imagined disasters of the future flit through my mind. Peace comes, as surprising as death.

11

Just the Facts

The day after Mother's funeral, Daddy called us girls together and said unhesitatingly, "I want to make one thing perfectly clear."

We waited, expecting to hear him describe his love for Mother one more time. Instead, he announced, "Your mother could not cook. People told her she could cook. She thought she could cook. But your mother couldn't cook. She used too much salt."

My sisters and I were too stunned by this declaration to respond. I searched for an explanation. Could Daddy be in a state of shock, so that his grief was coming out this way? I surveyed my sisters' faces.

Mary Ellen's hazel eyes revealed that she was hiding inside herself. Through the years she had developed a persona that represented her in the world when she was feeling vulnerable, and this girl was doing the job of being Mary Ellen.

Tall, elegant Patty was in therapist mode, determinedly aloof and ready to listen. Her pretty blue eyes were red-rimmed, however, and her usually immaculate manicure was chipped. She and her daughter Katie were inseparable.

Julie Ann's usually baby-fine skin looked ravaged from grief and surprise. She held her chin up as if someone had belted her, and she was ready for them to take their next best shot. Her beautiful auburn hair that ordinarily framed her luminous face was yanked back into a ponytail.

Instinctively, when Daddy began to re-create the story of Mother's life inaccurately, my sisters and I did not respond to his revisionist theories. Everyone knew that Mother was a good cook. In time, Daddy would remember this too.

Relieved of the burden of the message he felt compelled to deliver, Daddy signaled for me alone to follow him. We went upstairs to his room. A strange and unfamiliar odor permeated it. I puzzled over the nutty, sour scent, but I couldn't trace it.

Oblivious to the unpleasant aroma, Daddy went to Mother's dresser, scooped up her jewelry, and handed it to me. "Take this to your house and keep it safe. When someone dies, people get greedy. Some lying and stealing can go on. You hold onto this until we figure out what to do with it."

I inventoried the contents of my hand: one pair of diamond earrings, a four-carat diamond tennis bracelet, a two-carat diamond bridal set, an engraved watch, and a diamond pendant. Is that all that a lifetime produced? A handful of sparkling doodads and the unfair eulogy "She used too much salt."

Mother did not use too much salt! Solemnly, I took the jewelry home and put the collection of treasures in the box on my bookshelf headboard. A vase of roses stood next to it — roses I had brought home from the funeral. I really couldn't explain why I had done it, but when I had tried to get in the car after the funeral service, I couldn't do it. I couldn't leave. A blanket of roses covered my mother's casket, and I couldn't leave them. Someone asked me, "Do you need something?"

I pointed and said, "I need . . . ," but I couldn't say the word *beauty*.

A stranger said it for me. "She needs roses."

As if it were a perfectly normal request, as if I had just said I was thirsty, the message was passed along: "She needs roses." From inside of myself where I wouldn't let myself cry, I saw the hands picking the flowers from my mother's gravesite, and one by one the blooms were passed along to me. Even after I was finally seated in the car, the roses kept coming — peach ones, red ones, white ones, and yellow ones — until my lap was full of beauty that I hugged close. Only then could I breathe. Only then could I leave.

My sisters didn't say anything, but it made them mad. I think my

needing all those roses was to them a worse social trespass than if I
had cried hysterically at the funeral. But I didn't do it on purpose. I
just couldn't leave without some beauty to hold onto. Now there were
almost four dozen roses all over the house, and I kept going from vase
to vase to catch my breath.

Those flowers kept me company as the lonely days passed. The
subject of my robbing Mother's grave was ignored, but conversations
ensued about who should have which piece of Mother's jewelry.
Mother had once appointed the recipients of the pieces, but our memories of what she had said varied.

Who got what? Daddy now said that Mother's diamonds belonged to him, and that he wanted to keep all the pieces for a second
wife that he wanted to find as soon as possible. "It isn't good for a man
to live alone. The Bible says that plain as day," he declared.

My sisters were horrified and speechless. Daddy spoke bluntly,
without apparent feeling. He didn't mourn. My sisters stopped using
salt when it was their turn to cook supper. No salt! In my mother's
house! Were they trying to please him, punish him, or avoid Mother's
fate, fearing he might criticize their cooking behind their backs? I felt
separated from my sisters, my mother. My hand reached for the
saltshaker twice as often.

Time passed. We took turns staying nights with Daddy until he
shooed us all away. "I'm a grown man. I can stay here alone." We left
late at night and returned early in the morning to find him staring off
into space, not doing anything in particular. He seemed disoriented.

I figured he needed closure. "Do you want to go see Mother's
grave?" I asked. On the way, I offered him a milkshake or hot doughnuts from Krispy Kreme.

"Let's not spend our money," he replied, which sounded like him.
But he couldn't remember where Mother's grave was, and that wasn't
like him.

We went twice to the cemetery, and we had to have help finding
the grave both times. After the second trip, we stopped going.

Instead, he and I walked and talked in our city's park every day;
and finally, when he was in the right mood, I persuaded him that

while the jewelry technically belonged to him, he was as good as dead if he didn't give the girls Mother's jewelry.

Eyeing the prospective brides who were also walking in the park, he said, "I'm not the man I used to be. Not young. Not so good-looking. Not so smart," he added bluntly. "And then there's my heart problem. I'm pretty much used up. I'll need all my resources to get another woman. That includes money and jewelry. That's not bad. That's just the way it is."

Daddy still looked pretty good in his daily outfit of jeans and a white T-shirt, but his thinning hair cost him sex appeal. His blind green eye had grown cloudy. Neither one of us mentioned the crimp in his personal parts. I thought he was right in his assessment of his once-famous good looks, so I didn't argue with him on that point. I had another objective that I was trying to sneak up on. "You've got a really nice house and enough monthly income to feed and clothe the right woman. The wrong kind of woman would be attracted to the jewels you are wrongly using as bait. You don't want that kind of woman. Like a gas-guzzling car, she'd be too expensive to maintain. Give the girls Mama's jewelry, or you will end up with a woman who will want more than you can afford and daughters who will not forget the choice that you made."

Daddy stopped in his tracks. "You're smart, do you know that?"

"Yes, sir, I do," I said.

He pivoted around, as if suddenly recognizing where he was. "I used to beg your mother to walk with me in this park, but she wouldn't ever do it."

I stared at the creek that ran parallel to the walking trail. I didn't like for Daddy to complain about my mama, but I was too close to defusing the jewelry bomb, so I didn't argue with him.

"Go ahead and give out the jewelry any way you see fit, and that'll be that. You girls are all I have . . . right now."

I acted quickly, before he had a chance to reconsider. I called my sisters and handed out the jewelry the best way I could figure. I gave the most valuable pieces to Patty Kate and Julie Ann because they were younger. They had had less time with Mother. As the elder sisters, Mary Ellen and I took the smaller diamonds because we had more time and memories to hold onto.

After the jewelry was dispersed, Mary Ellen had a dream that worried her. She told me about it when we were sitting on the front porch at Mama and Daddy's house. "I was wearing Mama's earrings, and all of a sudden Mama showed up. I snatched those earrings off and declared, 'These are yours! I don't know how they got in my ears.'"

I understood that dream. It did feel as if Mother couldn't really be gone but was just away somewhere and might come back any minute. If she caught us wearing her jewelry, she wouldn't like it.

Julie Ann reported the next dream about Mother. "Mama was wearing a bright lime-green suit, and she looked beautiful, happy, and rested! Mother is all right now."

Patty dreamed about Mother so often that no single dream stood out. But they were always sweet dreams, and she was always comforted.

I never dreamed about Mother, but I did develop a strange sensation of never being alone. When I looked in the mirror, it was as if I could sense a presence beside me. After a while, I remembered that dream of long ago in which a small, gnomelike being stood hunched beside me in front of the mirror in the rehabilitation center. I didn't know who it was. The unanswered question nagged at me.

Our daddy jubilantly reported that he had seen Mother while he was wide awake. He was alone when it happened. In spite of his increasing litany of complaints about her, he was happy to see her. "Your mother was standing in the pantry, holding a can of LeSeur peas. I saw her plain as day."

I thought at first that God had been merciful and given Daddy a final vision of Mother, and I thought it unusual, but God does unusual things. The Bible is full of reports of God's mysterious activities.

But then Daddy reported that the television was coming on again by itself. Only no one ever saw it happen but him, and Mother wasn't there anymore to be leaving the TV on at night. I checked the batteries in the remote. They were good.

Julie Ann decided to come and stay with Daddy for a couple of weeks to see if she could figure out what was wrong with him. I was glad. I had been spending most of my days there, and having Julie Ann home would let me stay in my own house, where my work had piled up. Besides, Julie Ann was the most fearless problem-solver in the family. She had objectivity and strength; and though she accepted the benefits of peace promised through good dreams, she was a realist. If a dream contradicted the facts, Julie Ann sided with the facts.

I had not yet thought ahead to what the future would be, but I knew that Daddy could not live alone for long. I wanted Julie Ann's opinion. Though Mother's death had caused him to rally, impersonating his old self, during unself-conscious moments he was becoming spooky again. He drifted from room to room, often becoming a statue. The man who had always turned off every light when he left the room began to leave the lights on all over the house. Sometimes, if it was raining, he went to his toolshed and just stood in the corner in the dark, as if waiting for someone. But no one was out there. What was he doing outside by himself? Was this grief?

He needed company. He needed more company than just his daughters. But the women he spoke to in the park often bolted away from him. Where were all of Daddy's previous admirers? I thought of Miss Annie. Mary Ellen told me she had died some time ago, not long after her father did.

I was just getting ready to fix Daddy up with a woman from my church when I caught him on the telephone talking to someone. He hung up guiltily, as if he had been discovered doing something wrong.

She was the woman he used to know, he said. The woman he had told me about in the car the day we came back from the personal-parts doctor. He looked at the phone as if he wanted to pick it up again, and then he said, rubbing his chin, "She's still married. Has a bunch of children and grandchildren. That's good, I guess."

I sat beside him in Mother's chair. I wanted to ask Daddy if he had apologized for his earlier behavior, but I asked instead, "Do you still love her?"

He sat back on the sofa, pulling his leg up to balance himself. "Your mother is the only woman I ever loved. And she has left me."

"I'm sure that's how it feels," I commented neutrally, but inside, I was suddenly relieved. Okay. Here was the explanation. Daddy felt rejected by Mother, a phenomenon associated with death. He was expressing his pain by criticizing her.

"It's the truth. Your mother wanted to leave me, or she wouldn't have gone."

He saw it the way I did.

"Your mother is living in China with that man she always wanted to sleep with."

"Daddy?"

"But if she wanted to come back to me, I'd take her back, because Hosea in the Bible took that harlot back. God approves of forgiveness even when a wife has been an unfaithful slut. I'd take your mother back. She just got confused, or the devil tempted her. Anyone can fall prey to the devil. He's a wily bastard."

"Daddy?"

"If it weren't for my night-time family, I'd be here all alone."

"Daddy?"

"What do you want?" he asked irritably.

"What night-time family?"

"Oh, there's a little dustball that lives on the dining-room table now. He runs with a little man about two feet tall who wears a black cape and only looks up when he's holding his arm in front of his eyes, like this." Daddy brought his forearm to the bridge of his nose to illustrate. "They're the two who keep turning on the television at night. There's nothing wrong with the TV set, although it should have busted by now. Your mother leaves it on all the time, even when she has those domino parties. She only has them while I'm asleep because she likes to be alone with her brothers. She thinks I'm jealous, but I'm not. They wake me up, though. Then, when I come down here, they all hide. Skitter like bugs."

"Daddy . . . Mother is dead."

"You don't mean it! When did that happen?"

"Daddy. You know Mother died. We went to her funeral. Do you remember how they had the wrong shade of lipstick on her? Patty

made them change it." This was a fact of history. I had taken one look
in the coffin and expelled a great sigh of relief: *God, thank you. That's
not my mama.* All of my sisters reported the same relief. The dead
woman in the casket looked like Mother some, but that lifeless, waxy
woman was not our mama.

Still, Patty thought the shade of lipstick was wrong, and it was,
because Mama had always, always used Revlon Soft Silver Rose, and
someone had put a mauve color on her lips that went with her good
blue suit just fine, but it wasn't her signature shade. Patty tracked
down a mortician and extracted Mother's lipstick from her own purse
and directed a stranger to repaint our mother's mouth. Why don't we
tend our own dead? Why do we call a stranger to touch the lips of she
who gave us life and spoke words of love?

When my best friend's father died, they parted his hair on the
wrong side, and Guin could not allow her father to be buried like that:
"He always wore it combed from the other side." She made this observation woodenly, objectively, as if analyzing a situation that can be
fixed, but death can't be fixed.

Attempting to be helpful, I asked the receptionist at the front desk
in the funeral home to call the person who makes a dead person look
more like the person we used to know. She immediately opened her
desk drawer and pulled out a makeup bag, removed a man's comb, and
excused herself. She walked on tiptoe, as if the sound of her footsteps
might wake the dead.

My friend stood in the lobby waiting, but I followed the lady with
the comb. She went over to the casket where my friend's father lay —
my good friend, too — and she recombed Elmer's hair. With arms
lifted like angel wings, her body formed an arc, a covering of protection while she tenderly corrected the final image of the man whose
countenance represented a lifetime of unconditional love: *Father.*

"Why would you want to say something like that about your
mama?" Daddy's voice called me back to the present.

"Because Mother is dead. It's true. It's a fact."

"I saw your mother just the other day. She was standing in the pantry, holding a can of LeSeur peas. I said, 'Hello, Shorty.' That's a fact too."

It was a fact, in a way. He had seen her, and he had said those words.
"Did Mother answer you?" I pressed.

"Come to think of it, no, she didn't. But, you know, your mother's gotten so that she doesn't answer me a lot of the time. I'm used to her not answering me."

Without answering Daddy, I turned on the television and went to call his doctor to find out what to do. Dr. Givhan didn't have to think for long. He recommended that I take Daddy to see a psychiatrist.

From the Family Album . . .

My Mother's Child

He hovers in front of the rocking chair where I sit, holding his sleeping grandchild. The room is shadowy, so I cannot see his face. He bobbles in front of me, finally kneeling. My arms tighten around the small girl who is too old to be rocked, but Katie is sick, and I want to hold her.

"She looked like you," Daddy finally says. He doesn't mean that the child I'm holding looks like me. He thinks that I look like my mother when she rocked this child.

Daddy sits down clumsily on my right. I focus on the muted television. Accustomed to being accused of deafness, Daddy doesn't complain that he can't hear the TV. The images flash by soundlessly in the dark room.

Katie coughs, rousing momentarily. Then she nestles closer. Her long legs stretch out to my knees. "Harder," she demands. I bury my face against her neck, kiss the place my mother used to kiss, and rock us both.

"Your hair. The way you hold the baby. You. She . . ." Daddy, in a state of dislocation since Mother died suddenly of a heart attack, takes spells of telling me how I resemble her. I abide his commentary, not pleased, but not resentful either, for I exist in the company of my family members, whose needs sometimes cause them to mistake me for Mama.

When Steve Muzio, my preacher, paid his condolence call, I told him my biggest fear was inheriting my mother's life. Now I find most of my comfort in doing her work.

"What do you want to do about supper, Grandmother?" Daddy asks suddenly. His mind takes nosedives. When did someone last speak my name?

I don't correct him. Instead, I ask, "How about we open up a can of stew, Pa?"

"I like stew," he approves. "We can eat it in here while the news is on."

An hour will pass before the news comes on. Katie's mom will get off from work and come for her child. Daddy and I will have the same conversation several times before the stew gets warmed and eaten. Time will pass in this new, uneven way.

I am not impatient for the time to go by or particularly unhappy while the present minutes are lived so slowly. It isn't a desperate state — this rocking zone where I live in a constrained area, holding a child too old to be rocked while having repetitious conversations with a man whose mind has aged suddenly from shock and grief.

Katie, sensing that the day is reaching the point when her mother will return, yawns and stretches feverishly into consciousness. I caress her warm head and study her features, which grow more beautiful to me by the hour, as do my daddy's. Katie pushes my hand away, for this child takes after her grandmother in not liking to wake up.

This late afternoon I count her bad temper pure pleasure, for, like my daddy, I am happy to find my mother's likeness in anyone, no matter how it manifests itself.

12

Those Gray Areas

As we were going into the office of the preliminary evaluator at the psychiatrist's office, Daddy stepped back to allow me, a lady, to precede him. The admissions evaluator grew solemn and asked in the carefully modulated tones that are characteristic of how mental-health professionals talk to the inmates of the loony bin, "Sir, did you just see something that made you jump back?"

Daddy understood the implications of that question and laughed. He winked at me in a private code that meant the man we had come to see was an idiot.

We sat down, and Daddy answered some standard questions. *Who is the President of the United States? What season of the year is it?* And finally, *How much is 3 from 100?* "Not as much as it used to be," Daddy quipped, sitting back in his chair. He looked like his old self. His eyes sparkled. He was ready to talk business.

Then the quiet man in gray asked Daddy if he could pose him a serious question about a problem he needed to solve, and Daddy, trained by a lifetime of friends and neighbors turning to him for help in solving their problems, answered, "Fire away."

"If you had a pair of pants on, and you couldn't take them off your legs, how would you remove them?"

"Pull them up right over my head, so they wouldn't tear up." Daddy grinned at me and tapped his temple. "That's using the old noggin."

The man in gray made a note and asked, "Who is this here with you?"

"The little lady," Daddy replied, patting my knee. It was the way he had always patted Mama's knee. His fingers gripped my inner thigh. I shifted away.

"We need you to answer these questions," the man said, his eyes avoiding the placement of my father's hand. He tried to give Daddy a long sheet of paper containing the hundred questions, but Daddy wouldn't take it.

"She does all my paperwork," Daddy said airily. "She even writes the checks."

I did write the checks now. I hated the job.

The gray man pushed the sheet of questions toward me. "Would you like to help your father answer these diagnostic questions? Perhaps we can get to the bottom of what's wrong with him if we have more information."

"Certainly," I replied primly.

Daddy and I were excused, and we went to a room where I could read the questions aloud to him. He grew bored quickly. At about the tenth frustrating question, he said impatiently, "Just put down what you think is the truth."

I did. I answered one hundred questions as if I were Daddy.

When we returned to the gray man's office, he scanned the answers and calmly suggested that it was time for a visit with the psychiatrist, Dr. Haldol. That wasn't the psychiatrist's real name, of course. My sisters and I nicknamed him that because Haldol was his drug of choice: the popular chemical mix that erases night-time families or, in the parlance of psychiatry, hallucinations. Write a record of them and call it a story, and the hallucinations are breathed into life and become characters, and the person who tells the story isn't crazy — she's a writer. I saw the distinction. It didn't comfort me.

When Daddy and I were ushered into the psychiatrist's office, Dr. Haldol was very calm. He focused on establishing a connection with Daddy, making good eye contact and complimenting him on the color of his shirt. After a few more comments and questions, he asked Daddy, "Would you be willing to check in for a few days of tests?"

I could imagine many benefits of a brief hospital stay. Daddy's meals would be prepared, laundry done. Old girlfriends might hear that the widower was in the hospital, and they could come and visit him, reconnect. What a good idea. I urged Daddy to do it. "It might be good for you. They can listen to your heart."

"You don't have to convince me. I've been telling you that there was something wrong with me for years, but no one would listen."

"You'll just need to go to the main office to sign a few papers," Dr. Haldol said, his expression pleasantly benign.

Having reviewed Daddy's grade-A hospital insurance, the administrator assigned Daddy a large, private suite. It overlooked a fenced back yard. He was immediately scheduled to participate in group sessions in the mornings and afternoons, and, yes, there would be women there. Daddy acted as if he were going on some kind of singles' cruise. Only he never got to meet the women he envisioned as possible romantic partners.

The word "tests" means something very different to a psychiatrist than it does to a layperson. None of the vocabulary words that I knew had prepared me to understand that the word "tests" is a code word for giving psychotropic drugs to a man who is hallucinating.

How did I miss that? I was there in the office when Dr. Haldol spoke in his unthreatening tones and explained what we were going to do, and what I heard was that Daddy was probably depressed and suffering from sleep deprivation, and that was why he was hallucinating. "If we can help him get some sleep and address the depression, the hallucinations may go away. Then Jerry has a chance at feeling better," Dr. Haldol said. This optimistic view fit neatly with my hope that Daddy could have a new life.

Dr. Haldol mixed up a concoction that he swore afterward was a regular anti-hallucinogenic cocktail for a normal crazy person, but our daddy wasn't crazy by normal standards. The drugs knocked him out, and nothing could wake him up.

When I called my sisters with the news that Daddy was now unconscious, they were seriously and rightly alarmed. No one said to my face that I had taken a grieving man and almost killed him, but I wouldn't have blamed them if they had.

For the second time in a month, Julie Ann drove six hours from Memphis to see how she could help. Mary Ellen and her family were living in Tallassee now, a good forty-five minutes away, but she came faithfully to Meadhaven every day.

When you walked into the door of that hospital, the nurse on duty gave you the once-over and then asked you to sign in. My sisters and I dutifully signed in day after day until we were told to stop. "You only have to sign in once," the nurse said, as if that made perfect sense. It didn't to me. Did most people only visit once? Were my sisters and I unusual in our sustained vigil? Were we being assessed, just as our daddy was? Whatever the conclusions made about us, we girls were close by while Daddy was unconscious. We took turns in pairs watching him sleep.

One afternoon, when Mary Ellen and Patty Kate took their shift in the hospital room with Daddy, Julie Ann and I moved to a waiting room. After we had fortified ourselves with a cup of coffee, she told me a secret — what had happened to her while she was alone with Daddy during one of the recent nights she had spent with him at the dream house.

"Daddy came to my room in the middle of the night and knocked on my door. I'm accustomed to one of the kids needing something in the night, so I didn't think anything about it." She took a deep breath. "Daddy had a gun, and he pointed it at me. Liked to scared me to death."

"A gun?"

"A loaded gun. I scooted out of the bed and onto the floor, talking easy like they do in the movies when the man with a gun is acting crazy — just as if I were talking to a crazy man," she added, her forest-green eyes growing large.

"He is crazy. Or was. He may be dying now." I said the words dully. "I may have killed our daddy."

"Daddy isn't dying," Julie assured me. "When the medication wears off, he'll come out of it. Don't borrow trouble. We have plenty. Tell me what else the doctor said about what is making Daddy act so strange."

I repeated the words one more time. "He said that Daddy is a hypervigilant personality, always on guard, watching the house, which is why he's leaving the lights on and can't sleep. Said he's probably pacing the house at night. He told me that the sleeplessness caused him to have hallucinations, but they might stop if we could help him get some sleep. I thought they were going to give him sleeping pills."

"That diagnosis seems perfectly reasonable. The doctor just didn't understand that Daddy is hypersensitive to medication."

"I didn't know they were going to give him hard-core medicines. When they said 'tests,' I thought, okay, he's over sixty-five, he's been on medication for his heart problem for years, and he could use a physical. He's also become something of a hypochondriac."

"Our daddy's gone crazy is what's happened," Julie said bluntly. "Literally. Not cute, not funny, not Southern crazy. He's gone out-of-his-mind crazy. We might have to lock him up." She crossed and recrossed her legs. She had an active family, and being confined and separated from them put her under a strain.

"Patty Kate has been trying to tell us for a couple of years that something was wrong with Daddy besides his heart. Why didn't I ever really hear her before?"

Julie shrugged, then sighed. "He always said that if Mother died first, he would lose his mind. It's like a self-fulfilling prophecy. You don't suppose he's talked himself into going crazy," Julie theorized.

"He started losing his mind before Mama died. Did she ever tell you about how they played the baby game?"

Julie shook her head.

"Mother said that Daddy pretended that he couldn't put his clothes on, and she had to help him. Only maybe he wasn't pretending after all."

Julie sighed again. "Mother didn't tell me about things that bothered her. She wanted me to think that their life was wonderful."

"She didn't tell me about the baby game for a long time. I heard about it the day that she found the sack of missing quarters."

"Our mother is dead. Do you ever just say those words to yourself?" Julie Ann asked, and she slipped into private time, where the past feeds the present. She closed her eyes briefly. When she reopened them, I peered into the deep greenness of her gaze, and I saw that my baby sister was older inside than outside. Maybe she was older than I was.

"Mother is dead," I repeated, because sometimes I did taste the truth of that idea. But how could she be dead? She had always been here. In the other room. Nearby. She always claimed she'd never go anywhere.

"Mother is dead. And Daddy is crazy. What does that make us?"

"People sitting around talking to each other in a lunatic asylum."

Meadhaven wasn't really that. It was a place for the emotionally challenged, where people lived separately but under one roof. When they passed each other in the hallway, they nodded carefully, politely, the ways tenants did in the old apartment building my Daddy used to own.

It was always quiet inside Meadhaven, no matter what might be happening beyond the perimeter of its protective fence. Inside Meadhaven, the outside world was irrelevant. The focus was entirely on what made people mentally ill.

While my sisters and I waited to find out what was wrong with Daddy, we were given to understand that sometimes people go crazy because living with their family sends them over the edge. For a while, my sisters and I were looked at as if we were the germs that had caused our Daddy's illness. We simply ignored the unspoken suspicions that we were the likely accomplices in causing Daddy to have a nervous breakdown.

When Daddy finally did return to a kind of consciousness after a severe response to that first series of drugs, he was very different. He was taken off the heart medicine he had been taking for years to see if that could have been the cause of his acting strangely. His heart kept a normal rhythm, but there was an unusual presence in his eyes. He also displayed a new set of peculiar behaviors. And he paced and paced. Part of the reason that he walked incessantly was that he was lost most of the time. He couldn't remember where his room was. There were only two hallways and only two directions — there and back — but he couldn't find his room three doors down on the left. The aides finally had to tape arrows on the hallway walls pointing to his room and hang a sign on his door with his name: Jerry.

Daddy became Jerry in Meadhaven, and my sisters and I stopped being Daddy's girls. We became counterpart figures in the drama he was now destined to live out as a social outcast. He wasn't our daddy anymore; he was our crazy old man.

From the Family Album . . .

James Bond, Mr. Coffee, and Dr. No

A male nurse whose name was Mr. Coffee told us that we could help ourselves to coffee in the hospital's kitchen. "But it is decaffeinated," he added, almost apologizing.

He waited a beat for one of us to make a joke about his name, but my sisters and I are pretty good about not making the easy joke. Besides, decaffeinated coffee isn't funny to us. All four of us clasped our hands decorously in our laps, nodded, licked our carefully painted good-daughter lips, and said politely, "Thank you."

Then, after Mr. Coffee left the kitchen, we pulled out our private supply of real coffee and made ourselves some of the high-voltage stuff. We needed it. It took a lot of energy to keep Daddy company in Meadhaven, a hospital for the mentally troubled.

Our Daddy was sick in a new way in Meadhaven. For a while he was incapacitated from a doctor-prescribed drug overdose, but when he finally did wake up from a five-day nap, Daddy thought he was James Bond for a while. He never said he was 007; his actions just proved it.

As soon as he could walk again, he started looking for an escape from the doctor who had drugged him and then assigned jailors to watch him. The doctor who told him he couldn't leave was just some version of the enemy, Dr. No.

Daddy bided his time, patrolling the environment. Late one night after the bed check, he slipped through a gap in the back fence and made it on foot as far as the Baptist hospital next door, where a security guard there, espying a man in his pajamas with a name tag on his wrist, discreetly offered him a lift home in his golf cart. Daddy accepted, telling me the next day that I needed to pay the fellow five dollars for cab fare.

Back at Meadhaven, Mr. Coffee was waiting. "Jerry, you aren't supposed to leave," he told Daddy in the soft, measured tones that mental health care professionals adopt with someone who is losing his wits.

Daddy nodded the same way we girls nodded politely at the admonition that caffeine was forbidden in Meadhaven. He docilely allowed himself to be escorted back to his room, but he was just waiting for his next opportunity to pull a James Bond. This time, Daddy left with a group of people from India who were dressed in long robes. He crouched down in their midst and duck-walked right out the front door in broad daylight.

Daddy was caught again and brought back, and we were told about his latest exploit, as if Dr. No and his staff thought we might be the type of people to sue them for losing track of Dad. We weren't.

We girls listened to the report, our hands still folded politely, painted lips compressed, and after the doctor was gone, we looked at each other, glints growing in our eyes: Somewhere inside of Daddy, James Bond still lived. Maybe in time, the rest of him would come back too.

It was a sweet dream while it lasted, but it didn't last very long. For twenty-nine days Daddy was observed at Meadhaven. Like my sisters, I was there much of the time. One day Dr. No watched me while I kept Daddy company on one of his marathon walks. Up and down the hallway we went at a pretty good clip, back and forth, back and forth, with Dr. No at his station looking at me over his clipboard, shaking his head and smiling condescendingly. Finally he said to me, "Your daddy's not going anywhere this time. You don't have to keep him company."

Making a speedy turn at the doctor's desk, I called over my shoulder as we power-walked right back where we had come from, "Why wouldn't I keep him company? We've taken walks before that didn't go anywhere."

That doctor looked at me as if I were crazy. I didn't care. It was the beginning of a new kind of alliance and a shift in the way I saw authority figures: Scorn my Daddy, scorn me. "The nut may not fall too far from the tree," I muttered fiercely.

There was a lot of muttering on these marathon walks that went nowhere in Meadhaven. Occasionally Daddy glimpsed the security guard outside patrolling in his golf cart and asked me one more time, "Did you pay that fellow five dollars for that taxi ride he gave me?"

"Yes, Daddy," I said, which was a lie. I didn't pay the man any money, although I was keeping Daddy's wallet full-time now. Managing all the money became my job in Meadhaven. My sisters accepted this without question or complaint, and I thought that their response was generous — as generous as their other actions and reactions to the mystery of Daddy's illness and its symptoms.

We took turns keeping him company and going on walks. After walking miles inside Meadhaven, we concluded that no matter how hard we looked, we couldn't find the man we used to know as our father again. We all lost weight, however.

But a different kind of weight accrued: it was the weight of a new knowledge that the whole family had moved with Daddy into a different stage of living where causes and effects are not immediately understandable through logic.

It felt like the end of the world, and this time, not even James Bond could save us — or himself.

13

Good Girls Gone Bad

While Daddy was in Meadhaven, my sisters and I were learning our new roles and were still partially visible to the world populated by people who narrow-mindedly partner the truth with only facts. Nurses, doctors, and medical technicians love facts, and some are perplexed by love when they see it, and that's a fact. They often said, surprised, "You girls really love Jerry. We don't see much love around here."

And we confirmed politely that we did love Jerry. Patty translated this message, explaining that these medical professionals were not necessarily complimenting us. "Codependency is what they call it behind our backs. The implication is that we're addicted to his need of us."

One more word — *codependent* — was added to the mix of defining caregiving, where acts of love are praised and paradoxically, simultaneously, condemned. I began to learn that the world at large is an enemy of the mentally frail and the people associated with them. And though the world urges love, it often doesn't recognize it or really approve of it.

I loved Jerry. And I told Jerry I loved him.

Jerry heard me off and on, as he came back to life in his way. Once he was more alert, he began moving about in a crouch, examining the floor for pieces of lint and scraps of paper. Sometimes he secreted the little pieces of paper away and wrote tiny little notes in a script so

small I almost needed a magnifying glass to decipher them. They usually read "Save me."

I kept the collection of tiny little notes written on little pieces of
trash in my wallet, next to the poem Daddy had written to Mother
and placed in a new Bible he gave to her on their thirty-fifth wedding
anniversary. I liked to remember that at one time he wrote love poems
to Mother.

Just nine years before, he wrote this:

To the only wife I ever wanted, given in hope that it will help us
to spend eternity together:
    There is a long and winding road along which each must go.
It leads beyond the hills of time into the sunset glow.
Only for a little while our loved ones leave our sight,
For just beyond the hills of time, they wait in God's eternal light.

> With all my love,
> Jerry

During our long, endless walks up and down the hallway, I would
call up memories of the man who wrote these words. Sometimes
Daddy and I would pass rooms filled with people who were going
through a twelve-step program that addressed their addictions and
would ultimately lead to a cure. I looked longingly into those rooms,
wishing there was a room for us where we could hear a plan, follow it,
and come out whole.

There was no twelve-step program that addressed Daddy's problem. There was no cure, and my sisters and I knew it, and I thought
that somewhere inside of himself, Daddy must know it too. Just before
he was about to be released from Meadhaven, Jerry smiled tiredly up
at me and said, "I must be dying. You keep telling me how much you
love me."

When I didn't answer him, and I couldn't lie to him, Jerry said, "I
don't see why you and I can't have sex. You say you love me, and
you're a nice lady."

I died. Went right up to heaven to see Mother, where I reported to her what Daddy had said, and she didn't answer me, because she no longer cared what happened to me. In that moment my previous understanding of what had happened to Mother disappeared and was replaced with a sense that she had abandoned us. She had let herself die, had left me behind to live the life appointed for the Miss Annies of this world, and now I was one of *them*. I felt betrayed in that moment by both parents.

Jolted by my father's shocking announcement, I stammered, attempting to emulate the quiet tones of the nurses and doctors trained to talk to the mentally unbalanced. "Because I am your daughter."

Jerry waved that reason aside. "We don't know that," he said, watching his feet. His left foot began to wiggle back and forth, and he giggled, amused by himself. "You say you love me. Why can't we have sex? Who is it going to hurt?"

Who was this man named Jerry?

Had the stranger wearing my father's face and bearing his name asked any of my sisters this question? I thought ahead to his living with one of us full-time, and the idea killed me again. How many times can a girl die before they finally bury her with or without the right lipstick? A dead woman now, I found it easy to adopt a cold tone. I said very clearly, "I do not want to have sex with you."

He giggled and rubbed his hands together mischievously, as if he thought I was flirting with him. "Be that way, then."

"That's the way I am, and that's the way it is," I said. I laid down the box of Krispy Kreme doughnuts I had brought him and left the room without looking back. I got in my car and drove home, but when I got there, I didn't want to go inside. There were buildings called Daddy's house and my house, but neither one of them felt like home.

Often when I went back to Meadhaven, I had the same reaction. I sat in the parking lot in my car, staring over the dashboard, unwilling to get out. The man inside didn't feel like Daddy anymore. Periodically immobilized, I groaned the kind of prayers that never become words.

While I was groaning in the car — probably looking very strange to passersby — doctors continued to examine Daddy. Jerry was watched and talked to and scrutinized. More drugs were mixed up and, after a plan had been explained extensively to us girls and tentatively tried, Dr. Haldol called us in to render his final diagnosis.

We went to the office together, our good-girl lips once again carefully painted. Dr. Haldol looked at us gravely, his eyes serious. "My early hypothesis was optimistic but wrong," he began. "The diagnosis is depression. But that's only part of it. Depression is a sister disease of what your father has — Alzheimer's disease. It's terminal, but your father's body is in great shape. We've never seen a patient of his age with better muscle tone. He could live another twenty years. He just won't remember . . ." Dr. Haldol stopped speaking, waiting for us to ask questions. We didn't.

Daddy was dying. The only questions were unanswerable: how painful and how messy was it going to be, and could we girls manage him?

I didn't think so. Julie Ann lived six hours away and had major family responsibilities of her own.

Patty Kate was raising a child, and even though she lived near Daddy and me, I wasn't sure how healthy it would be for Katie to be exposed to too much more suffering at her age. She had already seen her grandmother die.

Mary Ellen lived in a nearby town, but she was coping with her own problems. Although she wanted to take on the job of providing Daddy with full-time care, I didn't think she'd last very long. But then, who would? Who could?

That left me, and I didn't want to become like Miss Annie.

We ignored the obvious questions in the beginning. Together we juggled our schedules informally. We investigated formal assistance options. We called hotlines and experts. We read books. Stubbornly, we tried to live in the old world where there were answers to questions and solutions to problems, not realizing that we had moved into a different way of being where accomplishment could not be and was not the goal — survival was. Taking care of Daddy was our reality.

We took turns staying with Daddy. But after a while, the adrenaline that keeps you energized for a short-term crisis dwindled, and we each began to feel the weight of the confinement and the sadness.

We missed our mother.

We missed who we had been as a family.

We missed our daddy, though he was present in his way.

We faced problems every day, and we instinctively wanted to turn to him for help in finding a solution, only to remember in that moment of surprise — and sometimes, anger — that he was the one causing most of the problems.

In general, he was unaware of so many tensions, but occasionally he came back to a closer version of who he had once been with flashes of understanding. These crystalline moments triggered a homesickness so great that the force of it felt like a punch in the stomach. Before we could adjust to the idea that a part of who he had been was still present inside of him somewhere, that aspect disappeared, and another piece of a personality that we didn't recognize took its place.

It was a different way of living together. It was a time of learning to trust our own judgments rather than obeying the rules that our parents had taught us. It was a time of reading books that were supposed to describe what it was like to take care of a man with Alzheimer's — only the books didn't really tell the whole truth. We didn't, either.

When someone asked how Daddy was doing, we said, "He's fine."

How can you explain the ways a person can come and go in the blink of an eye?

And when someone asked, "How are you?" we sidestepped telling the whole truth. Usually we said something like, "I'm still sleeping at Dad's these days." And we managed to smile tightly, as if we were really sleeping at Dad's.

As Mother had known for years, sleeping was hard to do with Daddy in the house. Daddy paced the house at night, fueled by an energy arising from hypervigilance. He patrolled. He scouted. When I stayed there, he rattled the doorknob of the big back room where I slept. He always said he wanted a peanut-butter sandwich. I always got up and made him one.

When I passed him in the dark laundry room that connected my sleeping room to the kitchen area, I growled deep and low from my diaphragm like a mean watchdog, alerting him to stay back. There, in the dark shadows of the night, he grinned at me lasciviously as if I were Mother, and I began to say, as if I were Mother, "Leave me alone. I have a headache."

Daddy's testosterone impulses eventually were translated into impulses of violence. He had already punched one fellow at Meadhaven — an aide who was only trying to shave him. The doctor warned us that when a man displayed violent tendencies, no facility would take him on. I realized that if Daddy's anger went unchecked, it meant that we didn't have a back-up plan for the time when our own energies might fail.

I paid attention to the tension building inside Daddy. Before he ever struck out at me, I could feel him needing to hit something. He slapped at me a few times, and one day, when we were in the bathroom and I was helping him brush his teeth, he mistook my handing him the toothbrush for an overture of aggression. He shoved my shoulder with his fist and warned, "Stay back, damn you!"

I backed out of the bathroom in small steps. He came after me, his eyes locked on mine, his anger growing, feeding on my mounting fear of him. He saw me cowering, backing up, and I knew, I knew instinctively in that instant that if I let him bully me even this one time, some part of him would store that victory inside and attempt to repeat it. Then, one after the other, he would attack my sisters when they were vulnerable or tired, and the baby, the baby, Katie, a four-year-old now who didn't know how to sidestep a crazy grandfather. . . . I thought of him ever being alone with Katie, and that was all it took.

I braced my left arm in front of me, lowered my head like a football player getting ready to rush an opponent, and I watched my father's number-one helper — me — run into Jerry. Adrenaline helped. I surprised him, pushing him against the wall. I declared in a commanding voice that I did not know was in me, "You ever hurt me or my sisters, and I'll make you sorry you're alive."

My threat was vague, as I meant it to be, because Jerry was paranoid enough to come up with an envisioned punishment far worse than anything I could carry out. He tested me a few more times; and when he did, I released the Rocky persona inside of me that I didn't know was there till she was needed. I didn't have to use force again. I just had to sound like I would. Eventually the bully in Jerry gave up. When the sexual and violent manifestations of this stage finally receded, I rejoiced — even as a new set of symptoms and strange behaviors emerged.

Day by day, stage by stage, my sisters and I navigated the different dimensions of Alzheimer's disease. It was an unrelenting series of problems to be solved that our parents had not prepared us for. I learned this lesson for myself: *If you don't like this stage of Alzheimer's, don't worry. It will pass. But another one will take its place.*

From the Family Album . . .

Prisoner of Love

Daddy wants to hit me. Sometimes when he passes me, the hairs on the back of my neck rise, and I arch away from him. I do not work at my computer anymore because when I do, my back is exposed to the living room, which is one of his thoroughfares. I do not trust the nature of his passing. He could sneak up on me with the rolling pin that he keeps beside his bed for protection.

My father is committed to self-preservation, which is one of the reasons he patrols the terrain of his house. Although he has the excuse of Alzheimer's disease (one of the symptoms is a restless roaming), I know that he is also guarding this place. He has been guarding it for years. "I'm not the kind of fellow who can sit still," he used to explain when my mother, weary of his circling the table where she played dominoes with her brothers, would admonish, "Can't you light somewhere?"

Now more than ever, Daddy cannot sit still. He cannot rest peacefully at night, and they have a name for this symptom too — it's called Sundowner's Syndrome. But what any caregiver who has known the patient a very long time can tell you is that many behaviors that are associated with the symptoms of this disease often can be traced backward in the patient's history. Restlessness was as much a part of my daddy's nature as the impulse to violence that he learned to control.

There are many family stories of Daddy's manly youth, when he pummeled someone for his own good. And stress sometimes made him tip over into violence. Once, when we girls were all small and Daddy was holding down three jobs and rarely slept, he became enraged over something and beat the plywood door to the living room off its hinges. Mother vacuumed most of it up and made him quit the third job right afterward. Now the paranoia and disorientation of Alzheimer's are feeding his stress, which triggers his violence. Occasionally he wants to punish his caregiver — me.

For caregiving is my crime against him. To him, I'm the jailor — the woman who makes him eat and bathe and brush his teeth and go to bed and to the bathroom, where he protests the chore of relieving himself.

Even as I appraise the dark side of my father's violent nature, which has the excuse of a disease, I judge myself: I do not always like myself, but I am surviving. It is a different gauge of what is acceptable behavior.

In this caregiving season, I have developed a healthy respect for the interior selves that live below the surface of us all. I operate out of intuition as much as reason and exercise the brand of guardedness named by lawyers as self-defense and diagnosed by psychiatrists as hypervigilance. When my sisters and I heard Daddy's diagnosis, we thought that in the naming of the symptoms there would be a solution. There wasn't. There were only the captions of changes in behavior that are supposed to mark the early deterioration that ultimately will end in death.

〻 The time frame of the disease's progression varies with the individual, but people grow old fast about the same way with this disease. At first people with Alzheimer's forget details. They don't quite remember locations. Get turned around easily. As their sense of direction fails, a restlessness sets in. An Alzheimer's patient paces the house, looking for an escape from his mental haze or searching for what he has lost.

Someone who has just been labeled "caregiver" is usually right beside him. Each is looking for something that cannot be found.

‣I live on guard, vigilantly monitoring the progress of my father's disease, grieving over the loss of my father's identity, even as I am inwardly railing against the injustice of being not his jailor but, like him, a prisoner of love.

14

Cain's Chapel

It is probable that one day I will be arrested for murder — for killing my father. My daddy will finally have a fatal accident I can't
predict or prevent, but it won't look that way. The police will come to
my door, invite themselves in, and ask me a few questions that I will
answer dispassionately. Though I know they will be assessing my
emotional state, I will not be able to force tears from my eyes. After
making copious notes in their little flip-top books and studying me
carefully while pretending to look around (I won't be making a very
good impression), they will take me downtown, where we will await
the coroner's report. If it is in any way inconclusive, I will be booked
for murder.

I imagine this happening, wondering what life will be like behind
bars. Probably a great deal different, for though I joke with my friends
that I am a prisoner of love in caring for my ailing father, actually I
have some liberty. I have a telephone. The mail comes six days a week,
bringing catalogs for people like me, who shop from them. We are not
a glamorous group of people, but we are a target market: we are
housebound caregivers.

I have called the 1-800 numbers in the middle of the night, surprised when someone answers, even more surprised when that person
doesn't think it unusual that there are women like me who are awake
and shopping throughout the night for garments we can only wear at
home. Like my mother, whose name is on these catalogs that come to

the house, I order inexpensive jeans with elastic waistbands because I don't know what size I am anymore, and I buy colorful sweatshirts and T-shirts. I have an insatiable appetite for pink and orange! I also often order sweatsuits for Daddy to wear because they have elastic waistbands — no snaps or zippers — and can withstand many washings.

I buy socks in a size that both Daddy and I can wear, because we go through a lot of them, and I don't have the energy to be sorting out which socks belong to whom. I buy white slipper socks with non-skid bottoms, because Daddy has a tendency to tumble, and sometimes when I try to help him keep his balance, I too need the extra brace of traction those rubber soles provide.

As much as I like those slipper socks, I dream of ordering pretty clothes for myself, like an evening dress in plum with a full skirt and a matching gold lamé wrap that I have my eye on. The picture in the catalog also shows the right shoes and the earrings that match.

"What do you think of these earrings?" I ask Daddy, holding out the catalog for him to see. I don't think he really understands me or even hears my question. He is inside his own world — but he comes out of it suddenly to slap at the new blue sofa I sit on because he thinks it cusses.

"Who's this here?" he accuses, kicking at it.

"That is still just a sofa. It's not anybody," I explain one more time. I have learned many fancy and polite names that are attached to Daddy's dementia, but I just call him crazy.

He roams physically and mentally. His states of awareness come and go, as do his paranoid delusions. Yesterday he had me call his brother-in-law. When Uncle Joe-Joe out in Arizona answered, Daddy whispered hoarsely into the telephone, "Murderer! Murderer!"

I took the phone away from Daddy, and Uncle Joe-Joe whispered in my ear, "Things don't sound very good over there, Daffodil." I crumpled, slipping to the floor at the sound of his voice. No one had called me Daffodil in a long time. I didn't even know I had missed it.

I held the phone tenderly, my eyes closed. "He's sick," I said meekly. "Don't mind him." I hung up the phone as soon as I could because Uncle Joe-Joe made me so homesick I couldn't bear it — so familiar, so far away. Then, pushing myself up to stand again, I fixed Daddy and me some hot cocoa, which we drank while we watched a rerun of *The Dick Van Dyke Show.* I wondered if Mary Tyler Moore might look good in my plum-colored dress.

My Uncle Joe-Joe called back later, after the show, after the cocoa, after I decided that Mary Tyler Moore probably didn't look good in evening gowns, which made me feel a little better.

"What can we do to help?" Uncle Joe-Joe asked softly, from far, far away. He thinks that his geographical location is the only measure of the distance between us, but he doesn't understand. He lives in the land of good clothes and fresh produce. I long for fresh fruit and vegetables, but I cannot go to the store often enough to keep them in the house. We eat canned fruit. Frozen vegetables. It's a major job just to keep the pantry stocked. He really couldn't help me with that.

"We're fine," I assured him. One of a caregiver's hardest jobs is to reassure people that she's fine.

"Call if you need me," he said.

I nodded yes before I hung up.

"Honey? Honey? Where are you?" I hear my daddy calling from the bathroom, where he has trapped himself between the tub and the toilet. Again.

I hear him beating his head against the wall. He hopes the wall is a door that will open if he strikes it long and hard enough. And that's how it is going to happen: He's going to knock himself out, fall hard, break his neck on the tub, and the cops will come and accuse me of hitting him with a blunt object. Then they'll cart me off to another jail.

Before I rise, I lean my head back against this sofa I ordered over the telephone from a newspaper circular. They delivered it for forty dollars. I worry that people might think I am spending Daddy's money frivolously. They don't understand that the blue sofa is my only place to sit that's clean. I only bought it because Daddy has leaked all over most of the other furniture. I had to get rid of the chair where Mother used to sit; I couldn't get the smell of urine out of it. Goodwill carted it away for free. Goodwill is a caregiver's friend.

This new sofa is wonderfully cushy, and the colors are bright and pretty. When I saw it in the circular, I imagined how I would look sitting on it with a piece of embroidery, a ladylike task that one does in the afternoon before taking a refreshing nap and then spending two hours showering and getting ready to go out at night to a party where a plum-colored evening gown with a gold lamé wrap is in order. If someone saw me sitting on this couch holding my needlework, I might even look like a character from a Jane Austen novel.

"Honey!" Daddy's voice trails across space, a long way, coming not just from the bathroom where he has trapped himself but from that psychological space where sometimes my mother is still alive for him and where the furniture talks and frequently cusses.

I push myself up, hoping I haven't dropped the needle, only to remember suddenly that there is no needlework. They don't sell that in the kind of catalogs that come to my daddy's house. They sell infused maple syrup and bedroom slippers and throw blankets, overpriced because of the picturesque images machine-stitched onto the fabric, which is not particularly warm. I have three of these all-purpose throws with picturesque images, and I cover myself up in one as if it is a gold lamé wrap that matches a plum-colored evening gown.

I go to Daddy. He is talking to the bathroom wall. "Open sesame. Open says me."

Daddy is not himself at all today. By this I mean he is not any of the selves that resemble him. He is actually absent. I stare into his eyes, trying to name who I see, but I am bumfuzzled. There is no look in Daddy's eyes that suggests that he is the man who raised me to have walking-around sense. He is not my sisters' daddy, not my mama's husband, not a man with a Midas touch, either. He is this different man — a lost person wandering through the wilderness. As I stare at him, I suddenly have the strangest idea: The fellow in front of me is the man who has killed the man who was my daddy.

"There you are," he says, smiling a welcome.

"Yes, here I am," I say, holding the blanket tightly. I am chilled. There is a mirror in the bathroom, and I see myself in it, all wrapped up with my hair a mess and no lipstick on. I do not resemble any of the bright, smiling models on the glossy pages of my catalogs. I look so old. Am I only forty? My hair needs to be cut and colored. My hands are red and dry. I need a manicure. I miss being pretty. I lean forward and stare into my own eyes and try to describe what I see. I do look familiar, just not like myself. I turn, and just as I do, I catch a glimpse of myself looking at Daddy, and I recognize that sweet old girl: I look like Miss Annie did years ago when she stood in the doorway, staring wistfully at Daddy when he was young and beautiful.

I confront the image and accuse softly the girl who is letting the other me go: "Murderer. Murderer." It feels like the truth.

The blanket slips from my shoulders. I take the thin cloth and wrap it around the man who wears my daddy's name. I tuck it under his chin, gripping the cloth so that I can lead him gently back to the sofa that he sometimes thinks is my lover.

"Where have you been?" he asks.

"I am right here," I declare firmly. "I am always right here, and I will stay right here as long as you need me."

I cast another glance at myself in the bathroom mirror, and suddenly there I am again. The eyes are right, the expression true. The chin juts up, determined. I am still his number-one helper.

"I know the difference between frozen vegetables and fresh," I announce brightly. My voice echoes in the small bathroom.

My Daddy's brow furrows. "I don't like corn," he replies seriously.

I lead us out of the small room and back to that other place where another blanket is draped over the small sofa that does not speak to me.

From the Family Album . . .

When Sofas Curse

Arms flapping excitedly, Daddy rushes over to the new blue sofa and exclaims, "I'm not going to have that kind of language in this house!"

Crocheting, I reply tranquilly, "I haven't said anything."

His eyes narrowed skeptically. "This guy here," he says, kicking the loveseat. "He hasn't been swearing?" Daddy repeats the expletive without embarrassment.

"No, sir," I say. "And this is no gentleman. It's just a small sofa, and it doesn't talk or swear."

Daddy's worried expression collapses instantly. He believes me when I point out that he is hallucinating. For him, sofas swear regularly. Specters only he can see stand at his bed during the night and watch him. Sometimes when I deliver clean clothes to his closet while he is napping, his head rises, catlike, off the pillow, and he watches me enter his room.

When he sees me, I explain slowly, "It's just me. A real live person. Your daughter."

Often he does not reply, not always believing that I am real. We lapse into a strange staring contest to determine whose idea of reality is reality. I usually blink first — that is, I continue toward the walk-in closet where I store his clean clothes. The next day he might very well claim that a fellow named Bill was in his closet moving his clothes around. I hear lots of stories about Bill, and don't know how one of Daddy's apparitions gained the name, for in the forty years that I have been this man's daughter, I have never known him to have a friend named Bill.

I consider this matter seriously. It is irrational, I know, but being able to find a real-life reference for one of Daddy's delusions makes the vaporous idea more tolerable for me. I persist in it. Like an emergency worker stacking sandbags against the rising waters of a flood, I try to build a safety wall for us by deciphering Daddy's hallucinations — by trying to understand his world.

I feel the same way about trying to interpret my world to him. "All this washing means that you will have clean sheets on your bed," I explain one more time.

"I do not care a thing about clean sheets," he says. It is such a nice, clear sentence. I stop and bask in the lucidity of it.

Since Mother died, Daddy cares little for the creature comforts of our life here. If I were to track this state back to a point in real time, I would trace it to the third week after Mother died, when we were finally able to change the sheets on their king-size bed. When the last fragrances of Mother's hairspray and Oscar de la Renta were washed away, some part of Daddy's will to be here drained away.

And after the sheets were changed, he refused to sleep in their bed. He didn't come right out and say he wouldn't, for he is a congenial fellow, and most of the time a blunt refusal like that is not part of his nature. Instead, he said that the bed kept throwing him out. He couldn't sleep till it was dismantled and the double bed from the spare room was reassembled in its place.

Daddy sleeps there now, often curled up sideways around a king-size pillow that is roughly the size of my absent mother. On my journeys to the closet, I have seen him pat the pillow and murmur to it when he thought I was only one of the vaporous images of his mind that happens to do the laundry.

We live together in this quirky rhythm, no longer giving and receiving hard information, which is something I miss in my father, for he used to know a lot of what other people considered facts. He may still know more than he can express, but his speech has deteriorated. His words are often jumbled. Frequently his conversation seems like an odd assortment of synonyms and soundalike words that don't often successfully communicate what he intends.

Like a mother who learns the language of an infant, I fancy myself Daddy's translator and claim to be able to decipher his mysterious language, although privately I wonder if I don't impose a meaning upon his speech and the way his mind works that is nonexistent. Am I a gifted linguist? Or is the explanation darker: Will I wake up one day in his world of specters and cursing sofas?

This morning, when I delivered Daddy a cup of coffee sweetened just the way he likes it, he grinned happily, slurped, and asked, "Do you see that sack of potatoes walking toward us?"

"No, sir," I said, and I did not add that I wish I could because it must be tiresome to be told you're wrong all the time. And then, because I can no more stop myself from asking than Daddy can quit seeing images that don't exist for others, I ask, "How could somebody who has just phrased that question not realize that there is something wrong with the idea of a sack of potatoes that walks?"

The man who once taught me how an air hose works in a car replied quite clearly, "Don't get huffy. It's not like I saw more than one."

15

Morning Has Broken

He sleeps diagonally across the low double bed, his feet hanging off the edge. His hands fret with the blue cover, and occasionally he mutters. I finish mopping up the different pools of urine that he created during the night, laughing softly because, after all this time, he was right: the flood did come. Every day begins with mopping the floor, and then putting the cleaning equipment back in the closet, even though we will need it again later in the day.

I wash my chapped hands and then sit behind him on the corner of the bed near his head. Outside, work on two new houses progresses, built on the two lots that had been reserved for my sisters but which we have finally determined they will not need. It is a time of paring down rather than building up, and the two vacant lots have now been sold. I am not as sad about it as I might have been once upon a time.

I lean over and kiss Daddy's forehead. "Do you want a cup of coffee?" He doesn't seem to understand. I press my face against his whiskery cheek and sit back and recall the flood of prayers I have uttered in this room, late at night after reading my Bible and wondering what God was up to in our lives. A lone bulb on the front porch of one of the new houses still glows. Up and down the neighborhood, dogs bark in a series, as if passing a message to one another. Daddy's brow furrows as if he senses danger.

"Everything is all right," I whisper. The tone of my voice is familiar to him, and I hope that, like a familiar melody, some part of me reaches into where he is and brings him comfort.

He receives most of my ministrations passively, unlike the man I once knew — the man who was greatly opinionated and vigorous and knew just how to do.

Now he says, in a rare moment of speaking, "I don't know your name."

Without taking the time to let that pain pierce my heart, I reply, "God knows our names. That's all that matters."

"God," he replies, and I do not know if that is a single-word prayer or a Job-like lament.

"God be praised," I respond automatically. I rise and go to the window where I can watch the work progress outside. The workmen are like all the construction workers I have ever seen — unafraid to make a mess. In the building process they have cut my waterline four times. It hasn't mattered. Waterlines can be fixed, pieced together and glued. The water tastes bad until you run a fresh gallon through the line, but then it's safe to make coffee again. I feel sentimental about the kind of problems that can be solved.

"I've got fresh coffee," I offer once more to a man who appears to be unconscious now, but I have discovered that he hears me later rather than sooner. What is required from me is the ability to wait. It isn't patience, really. This is a new kind of faith.

I didn't have this faith when Daddy was first diagnosed with Alzheimer's. I was afraid of this labor. Not afraid I couldn't do it. Afraid I could and then would find myself trapped inside a house living a life that didn't really belong to me. But in the midst of this great confinement, I have discovered a kind of liberty that I didn't know existed until I was trapped on all sides with nowhere to go and no one to save me. Along the way, I have found a new dimension to my life, discovered while Daddy lost his identity that this woman I've become is only a temporary emanation of personhood.

Like seasons, people have different times to be and different ways of living in that time. Right now, I've learned how to be content with nothing but a broken heart and the remains of a man who is dying slowly, messily, unpredictably.

He can look like this — prone, unconscious — and be like this for hours, only to rouse to consciousness, eat, be cleaned up, and begin his incessant roaming. That used to bother me, but now I see it as aerobic exercise, and I rejoice.

If I didn't know how he could change, I'd be afraid. I used to be afraid all the time. Went to sleep in pain and fear. Woke up in dread and fear.

Now I bless the name of God and call the time here a season of love. I believe in love, I trust love, though I know love can be a killer.

More construction workers arrive to work on the new houses. I admire the brick they have chosen for the facades. I think it's a good thing for people to be building new homes for growing families because there is a season for growing just as there is a season for dying. It is their season to enjoy the woods that was our family's land.

The saws and hammers are loud, and the sounds of work cause Daddy to groan in response.

I place my coffee mug down on the floor, and I go to him.

"Are you able to stand?" He strains, but he can't command his feet to move. "I'll fix your breakfast now if you're hungry." He can't answer me.

I put my hands underneath his arms, and I pull up to remind him which way up is, because he doesn't remember. "On the count of three," I say, but I don't think he understands my words. Still, he knows the tone of my voice, the pacing of my speech. My talk is a prod that is successful as communication in spite of the words, not because of them. Once he is up, I put my arms around him, and we embrace. This gives him time to find his center of balance. Then I peel down his soiled britches, clean him up with washcloths soaked in warm water, and redress him. He keeps his eyes closed, as if a part of him understands what's happening and can't face it.

When he is clean and dressed, we move across the room slowly, toward the kitchen. An hour later, breakfast done, I ask if he will let me shave him. He nods, his eyes unable to connect with mine because he cannot tell where the sound of my voice is coming from. He often does this: turns his head exactly away from the direction of the person speaking to him. But then, he usually mistakes left for right, and a change in flooring for a deep hole that people fall through. He walks around shadows on the floor, afraid of them.

After I've balanced him on a tall stool by the sink, I soap his face, lather it, and shave him. Next I clip the hair in his ears, clean out his nose, and then take a clean cloth and, stooping, wash between his toes. It is always sticky there. Suddenly a spit bomb lands on the top of my head, and I bounce up, though I shouldn't be surprised, because this has happened before.

"Don't spit on me," I admonish harshly, the tone of my voice unspeakably cruel. "I'm sorry," I apologize immediately. "I lost my temper."

The cloud lifts. "You have every right," he says clearly. "You are under a terrible strain. I thank God for you every day."

I sway with the force of a love returned so unexpectedly, and I kiss his cheek and apologize again, though it isn't necessary. I need to say it more than he needs to hear it, because our love is alive and in many ways different from the old way of love that required so much conversation and characterization and explanation. We live in a season of Love is.

"May I help you with a shower now?" I ask.

"Certainly," he says rather formally now. Because he is still unsteady on his feet, I grip his waist and hold my father's hand, which squeezes mine so tightly that I will have to physically peel back each finger when it is time to let go, but I know how.

From the Family Album . . .

The Close Shave

Like a blind woman learning a man's features, I hold my father's face, caressing his cheeks as if my fingertips need to know the length of his beard before I can shave him.

In the meantime, the faucet finally produces hot water. I place a steaming cloth over his face, massage his eyebrows, dry his eyes, the insides of his ears, the back of his neck. Although I have already washed his hair, I rub his head briskly with a hot cloth. Like a satisfied cat, he wriggles, insinuating his head into the palm of my hand. His shoulders drop as he gives in to the long, slow sigh that escapes him.

"Do you want to shave yourself, or shall I?" I ask, knowing the answer.

It takes a few seconds for this question to penetrate his consciousness. The answer finally comes to the surface. "You," he mumbles through the cloth. Speaking slowly, he adds a rare commentary: "I love the way you do it."

I begin to hum "Indian Love Song," an old Jeanette McDonald and Nelson Eddy number. The washcloth is dunked and squeezed and placed on his face repeatedly, a technique I learned from a real barber — one of the old-fashioned kind who invests thirty minutes in shaving a man. I took my father to the barber three times before I learned how to do this job. And now I do it right: slowly, ritualistically, spending time with heated cloths and aloe cream, and I always use a sharp blade. I am extravagant with razor blades, because what's money compared to my father's comfort?

Beginning at his sideburns, I work down the chin, the neck, and up the other side of his face. He stays silent, his eyes closed, his body folding up in front of me. He is barely standing, and I would sit him down if I didn't need him to brush his teeth afterward. Whenever I can get him near water, I try to put the toothbrush in his hand. Even though I am intent on my ultimate purpose of getting his teeth brushed, I do not rush the shave because Daddy likes the routine so much, and this is, I believe, one of the rare moments in his day when he is relaxed.

My sisters think I spoil Dad. Other experts advise me that I am supposed to let him do as much as he can for as long as he can. But I have discovered that all of the experts who counsel people like me on how to shepherd an ailing man through a frustrating day don't acknowledge that human beings need a little coddling. I chuck the rules for caregivers and emancipated women when I shave Dad. My instincts tell me to spoil him with warm washcloths and familiar motions repeated in the same way so he won't be startled by a darting hand flashing past his one good eye. When I shave him, I forget that he is dying slowly and that all my efforts can't stop it. During the shave, I let myself love him wholly while his face is in my hands. My hands work to memorize his features, take his likeness into my grasp so that I will never forget the feel of his living presence after he is gone.

When I finish shaving him, I apply a cold cloth to his face and say, "This is how Paul Newman stays so good-looking, except he uses ice cubes, I think." Daddy shivers. As soon as the cloth comes off and his eyes open, I put the toothbrush in his hands, and he brushes his teeth before he remembers that he finds this task objectionable.

"Rinse," I say. "Are you ready for a glass of cranberry juice?"

Bob Barker is on. I lead him to the sofa, where I help him center his bottom over the couch and settle him against the heating pad for his back pain. My whole body is a tool I use to maneuver him. I am proud of the physical strength I have that can be used for his care.

Sometimes we miss the first game on *The Price Is Right* because sitting down takes a while, and he can't differentiate his right hand from his left any more than he can figure out the reverse image of himself in the mirror. Other people with opinions about how I take care of Daddy know about his physical limitations, but critics still opine from time to time that Daddy should shave himself. And they shake their heads at me and cluck disapprovingly, "You're doing too much."

Maybe, maybe not. One person's terminal illness may simply kill more than the person who has the disease, I want to say. Maybe this is how much labor a disease like this costs not only the patient but also the family. But I don't usually say this, because I know that their criticisms of me are based not so much on concern for me as on fear of the future. They are afraid, I think, of how much will be needed before this episode of Daddy's illness is over. It's their survival instinct that is surfacing out of fear.

I have a survival instinct too, but I am no longer afraid of what the cost of Dad's illness will be — of spending my life this way. His disease won't really kill me. In many ways this caregiving sojourn has blessed me with an ability to live intensely the most ordinary of moments. I am very much alive in a way that I never have been before. I don't know how I reached this plateau of peace — I'm just not afraid. I know who I am, and I don't think that loving my father with my whole heart will ultimately cost me my identity. Rather, I think loving him has helped me know myself better.

Ironically, what exhausts me most about Daddy's illness is not doing the work that caregiving requires but confronting the series of opinions which are delivered as regularly as the commentary Job's friends offered to that tragic hero when he endured a period of travail. Relatives, friends, health professionals, and even strangers I encounter often feel free to judge me and what they call my codependent traits: They say I am afraid to live my own life — that I am unable to let go of one parent because I've lost the other. I think I know what they mean. I tell them that at some level they could be right about my being unceasingly concerned about Daddy's care, but I see it differently. Daddy is very sick, I love him greatly, and I just want to make him as comfortable as I can for as long as I can because he won't be here forever.

In a world that is constantly assessing levels of dysfunction within society and its families, how crazy is that — really?

16

Life at The Rock

When I climbed up on a chair rather than use the stepladder to change a burned-out lightbulb on the front porch, I broke one of the rules I was raised to observe. So it didn't surprise me that the bulb didn't twist out evenly as it should have. Instead, it broke off in my hand.

"Good night, Miss Agnes!" I muttered. At the same time, the plastic chair I was precariously and wrongly standing on shimmied beneath my weight.

The man who had promised that he wanted to be electrocuted in my place roamed right past me, oblivious to my position, not even stopping to hold the chair. I watched him shuffle on in a circle, his head down, as the breeze bathed my face. Automatically I closed my eyes and absorbed the feeling of the approaching autumn — my favorite time of year. "Lord, I'm going to need some help getting that lightbulb replaced," I announced as I stepped off the chair. It promptly tipped over, attesting to the true fact that it really wasn't a makeshift ladder.

Daddy turned toward me when I spoke, as if he thought I was talking to him. I wasn't, not really, although I missed him terribly, and sometimes when I talked to him, he talked back. But not today. He was inside his own world, where things must spin a lot, because he was walking in circles.

The phone rang, and I reached over and pressed the button on the cordless. It was the cable TV man, asking for directions. "You're not far," I assured him. "Take a left turn and drive down two streets. Then come through the open gate."

I walked past Daddy to stand in the driveway and watch for the installer. When I saw his white van in the distance, I waved with both arms. "We've got company," I told Daddy. He didn't seem to hear me.

When the cable man turned into the circular drive, I greeted him too warmly, as if he were a member of my family. Right off, I saw that he thought there was something peculiar about my exuberant welcome. He avoided making eye contact with me while he lifted out his toolbox. I know that look from strangers — nervous, assessing. I saw him wonder why Daddy was walking in circles.

"Daddy's taking his morning constitutional," I explained simply. I walked over and looped my arm through Daddy's to slow him down, and my old man gave me that one-eyed look that was part suspicion, part gladness. In that moment, Daddy wasn't quite sure who the lady was holding onto him, but he wasn't sure he objected, either.

"It says here that you want cable TV upstairs," the repairman said, reading from his worksheet. He used an official-sounding voice, louder than necessary, but I wasn't offended. He was just trying to keep some distance between us. Perfectly logical.

"We do," I agreed crisply.

He looked at me closely then, and I saw myself through his eyes. I was, quite simply, a mess. All of my own clothes were in the wash, so I was dressed in a pair of Daddy's navy stretch pants and one of his T-shirts. I wore one of his insulated red-flannel shirts too — it still made me feel safe. Completely illogical and also true. My hair was stringy and more gray than red. My hands were rough from washing countertops and mopping with Clorox.

In spite of my resolve to let the repairman keep his safe distance, I wore an astonishingly goofy smile, for we had company — real company. A man with a toolbox who could fix things. I grinned delightedly, foolishly, and asked him if he wanted something to drink.

"No, ma'am," he said, his eyes still averted from Daddy. "You've got expensive wall siding on the second floor, ma'am. I don't see how I can install a line upstairs without causing some damage."

"We want cable TV upstairs," I said, cutting to the chase.

"Even if I can do it . . ."

"We want cable TV upstairs," I repeated firmly. "Every single channel we can get!" It was what Julie Ann had told me to order before she came back to take her next turn with Daddy.

"We need every channel that's available while we're doing time at The Rock," she had said. "The Rock" is what she called the dream house now. I kind of liked it.

The man fetched his ladder from the van and placed it just where my chair had been on the porch. "You've got a really bad-looking lightbulb here, ma'am."

"It broke off," I said. "And I can't afford to get myself electrocuted right now trying to take it out myself. This old man needs me too much."

Silently the man took a pair of insulated pliers off his tool belt and gingerly gripped the lip of the bulb's base, twisting it out. Tears filled my eyes at the Lord's goodness in supplying help so quickly, but I brushed them back — you can't cry over the goodness of the Lord in front of strangers. They don't understand. They think you're crazy.

Instead, I leaned down and retrieved the good bulb I had brought out earlier and handed it to the man on the ladder. After he installed it, he climbed down without putting the light cover back on. I didn't mention it, but I sure wish I had said something to the Lord about it when I asked for help in the first place. *I must be more specific in my prayers.*

"Looks like I'll have to drill through the siding, and if I do, I can't promise you that you'll get a clear picture, because I'm going to have to splice onto a leg of the cable, and the signal will already be weaker."

"We want cable TV upstairs," I said.

He eyed me suspiciously, as if he thought I had a screw loose, and I giggled. I used to worry about how I looked to strangers, but now I figured if they saw me as imperfect, they were simply seeing the truth of us all. I saw people that way now. We were no longer divided into two definitive groups that inhabited opposite worlds: sane and crazy, whole and broken, strong and weak. The boundaries of strength and weakness had blurred for me, as had the behaviors considered normal and crazy.

This new perspective was really quite a gift. It had released me from the lifelong imprisonment of trying to look capable and strong — and sometimes, as in this moment, even normal. Now I was weak all the time with Daddy and constantly throwing myself on the mercy of God for help. I needed a lot of help — as much help as Daddy did.

Mostly I needed help keeping up this house, which continued to deteriorate even though it was an inconvenient time to be trying to maintain it. Recently the roof over the carport had begun to leak, and I had to have a new roof put on. The same guy who fixed the roof helped me change the tire on the riding lawn-mower while he was here. He was a one-armed fellow who was very good with his feet. I was impressed with his ingenuity and the way he shook my daddy's hand — understanding that there was something wrong with Dad but that it wasn't contagious. Some people treat Daddy as if he's a germ that can be caught.

After the one-armed man and his buddy — together they called themselves Three Hands Construction — fixed the roof and then the lawn mower, I asked them if they could take down the big mirror on the far wall in the living room — *no, not the pink one, that big one at the end* — because for a man who hallucinates, so many reflections can be something of a challenge to live with.

They went right to it, and while they worked I made a fresh pot of coffee and brought out a box of Little Debbie snack cakes, wishing I could offer them a butter-almond pound cake like Mama used to bake, but I can't make one these days. I simply can't afford to use six eggs in a cake because I can't count on being able to go to the store to buy more when I run out. I have the money. I just don't always have the time or the freedom to go.

The two fellows who took down the large mirror said no to Little Debbie, but they had a cup of coffee with Dad and me, although they both drank it standing up and kept one eye on the front door. But that was all right. I find in these days of living with Alzheimer's that I don't get my feelings hurt too easily, because most people are wounded or broken and trying their best not to let other people see. These days, people see pretty easily that I'm living at The Rock, where we will now have cable TV upstairs.

"Sign here," the repairman directed, after he had finished installing the line. He finally stepped close enough to hand me the clipboard and a pen.

He was a nice-looking fellow with a working man's hands and arms that were muscular and brown from splicing cable in the sun. I wondered if I had brushed my teeth that morning, and suddenly wished I knew for sure. Daddy's teeth were brushed, but I wasn't so sure about mine.

"Are you here by yourself?" he asked, as he finally risked making a personal connection.

I handed back his clipboard and pen. "No," I said. "We're together. And I have sisters." I didn't mention the Lord, because most people don't want to hear about the Lord even if they're Christians, which is strange. Crazy, even.

I didn't like the sympathy that suddenly showed up in his face, so I told him something he didn't need to know. "We've got a lady from a home health-care agency coming later today; and if we get approved, they're going to send somebody out three times a week to help Daddy get his bath. Wouldn't that be wonderful?"

"I reckon it would be," he agreed as he tore off the yellow copy for me. "There will be a charge on your next bill."

"And we will pay it," I promised, smiling. "Isn't it a beautiful day? Autumn is such a pretty time of year."

He looked around at the leaves that were falling from the many trees in the yard. "It's a big job to rake up all these leaves," he said.

"I suppose it is," I agreed. I hadn't even thought about the leaves yet. I wouldn't rake them up, though. I'd use the riding lawn-mower and cut and bag them.

"Give us a call if we can do anything else for you." When he heard himself make that offer, his eyes widened, as if he couldn't believe he'd been so shortsighted. He was in no hurry to come back.

"We've got everything we need right now," I said, smiling again. "Daddy, our company is leaving."

Daddy walked over slowly and held out his hand. The cableman looked confused, but because I was watching him, he took Daddy's hand and shook it. Daddy smiled so big that the man forgot to be afraid of growing old himself, and he smiled too. Then, like most people who come here, he left as fast as he could.

"He was the best kind of fellow," Daddy said, making a whole sentence all of a sudden. Then he made another one. "You're a good fellow too."

"Thank you," I said. Not long ago I would have explained that I was a girl, but that type of distinction didn't matter so much anymore.

"We got the lightbulb fixed today, and cable TV upstairs for Julie Ann, and there's a fresh box of snack cakes inside."

"Julie Ann?" Daddy said his youngest daughter's name, searching for the connection.

"She's a good fellow too," I said, as I looped my arm through his once more and led us back inside to what used to be called the dream house and now was mostly a house of prayer. Julie Ann called it The Rock.

From the Family Album . . .

Confabulation!

The kitchen sink was filled with suds and the few dishes that I'd decided not to put in the dishwasher. I plunged my hands into the very hot water and scrubbed the plates hurriedly, turning the water back on to rinse them one by one. It had been a while since I had drained a big sinkful of hot water through the pipes to clear out the grease, and I had decided to spend my hour off from taking care of Daddy by doing something useful. Something normal. Something that felt like progress. I was going to hand-wash some dishes and then rinse out the sink pipes.

The task helped me wait for Daddy, who was in the back room getting a washdown from a fellow named Oliver, whom the home health-care agency had sent over. Oliver was very gentle and very quiet, and I liked him. But I hadn't liked the woman from the agency who had interviewed me the day before, and who, after five minutes of being here, got a call on her cell phone and while on it whispered, "The daughter is showing some wear."

A polite woman would not have said that where a caregiver who's showing some wear could hear it. A polite woman myself, I ignored her tactlessness, allowing my eyes to glaze over when she ticked off Daddy's symptoms as if that meant there were also solutions for them. Sundowner's Syndrome. Hypervigilance. Paranoia. And when Daddy interrupted her to say that Mother was upstairs rolling her hair but when she came down, she'd make us all a pot of coffee, the woman offered me a smug smile and said, "You know what he's doing, don't you? He's confabulating."

"Making it up as he goes along?" I asked.

"Dementia patients do that to hide the fact that they don't know the answers to questions."

"Really?"

"Oh, yes," she said.

"Actually, Daddy's always been very hospitable," I explained. "He might not have the facts straight, because Mother is dead, but his offer of coffee is completely true to his nature. In that way, he is still himself."

She studied me, frowning as if that idea were so complex that it would require great thought. It wasn't a big idea, but it didn't fit into the world of facts where most people prefer to navigate, and so it made her uncomfortable. I smiled pleasantly and waited for her to hand me something to sign, which she promptly did. "The insurance will only pay for Oliver to come three times a week for thirteen weeks. But after that, there's always Hospice."

"Know all about it," I said, signing my name.

"Oliver will be here tomorrow," she promised.

And Oliver had come. Efficient. Polite. Quiet.

Where Oliver was quiet, Daddy was loud. He emitted another series of whoops, and one more time I walked to the back room to make sure that Oliver wasn't hurting my father. I stood in the doorway unobserved and watched while Daddy was being bathed very tenderly by a stranger. Oliver gently dried him off and then dressed him, humming an old hymn while he worked Daddy's arms into his shirtsleeves. Then he prepared to give Daddy a close shave.

That was my regular job, and I was good at it, but I could let go of that duty for a while. It would be my job again when it was my turn. In the meantime, I was catching my breath. That's what everyone said I was supposed to do during Daddy's bath time with Oliver.

The phone rang, and I hurried to it, snagging the receiver on my way to the sink, where I unplugged the hot, sudsy water and felt a great rush of pleasure in taking this normal preventive measure of cleaning out the pipes to avoid a grease clog later.

It was Julie, calling to see how Daddy was. He was whooping again, and she could hear it. "What is that noise?"

"What does it sound like?" I asked, taking a deep breath.

"Sounds like a Viking war cry," she said.

"Daddy's getting a bath from a man named Oliver."

Julie knew about Oliver, but she took a moment to digest the fact of the whooping. "Daddy used to like those old Viking movies."

"A Viking war cry?" I repeated the phrase. It pleased me. "Or he could be trying to sing Nelson Eddy's part in 'Indian Love Song.' Maybe he thinks he's singing a love song to Mama upstairs." I liked that idea, even though I still remembered that Mama wasn't upstairs.

"He's calling for help in his way, isn't he?" Julie asked suddenly. "He's afraid of Oliver, and he's calling for help, and he doesn't have any words today."

I nodded yes into the phone, a confession of betrayal: I had accepted help from a stranger who scared Daddy.

"You need to pretend he isn't afraid because you need the help of a stranger while you can have it, don't you?" Julie stated matter-of-factly.

I nodded yes one more time and whispered, "Oliver is very gentle, and he's doing a very good job. I would tell you the truth if he weren't."

"Okay, then," she said. "Daddy's a Viking, and he's enjoying that bath! Those are whoops of pleasure."

I giggled. "Yes," I agreed. "But there was a health-care professional here yesterday who would say that we are confabulating."

Julie ignored that. "What are you doing with this hour off?"

"Washing dishes. Cleaning out the kitchen pipes. I'm going to change the air filter next."

"Daddy would like that so much," Julie approved. "And if he knew everything, he'd prefer that Oliver bathe him."

I swallowed hard. "Yes, he would," I said, as the whooping suddenly stopped. I didn't go and look. I knew how Daddy would be. He would be still now and very deep inside of himself, where he hid sometimes when he was really afraid.

"I'll call you later," Julie promised, and we hung up as the smell of Old Spice filled the back room and began to permeate the kitchen. I hadn't used aftershave on Daddy in a long time. I had forgotten about it. But there it was: his signature scent. I inhaled it deeply as I went to the storage closet where the air filters were kept. I went to the thermostat, switched it to "off," hurried to the unit, and finished changing the filter just as Oliver rolled Daddy out in his special chair that was sort of like a recliner on wheels. Daddy was clean, dressed, shaved, and he smelled good.

Oliver picked up his workbag and headed to the front door as I called after him, "Do you want a Little Debbie snack cake?"

He grinned, his teeth white in his wide smile. "Maybe next time," he said. And before I could gasp "Thank you," Oliver disappeared through the door.

I wasn't sure if Oliver meant that or if he really meant he'd eat a snack cake with us one day. But, like so many pieces of conversation that we all have every day, the factual content didn't matter so very

much. The memory of Oliver's tender help and his smile stayed, and
there was Daddy, all clean and handsome and smelling good, and the
dishes were washed, and the pipes had been pampered, and the air filter was changed. I took a deep breath: those were the facts of the hour,
and I really liked them.

IV

HEAVENLY PLACES

17

Tell Me a Story

When I opened the door to throw our newest addition to the family — a real live dog named Rufus — a good-night bone, the biggest jumping frog that had ever lived in or outside Calavares County leaped into my life. He hopped straight through my legs into the kitchen.

Was he real? Had I imagined him?

"Can I keep it?" Katie screamed happily.

"Frogs belong outdoors," I said, tight-lipped. Then, looking skyward to God, I mouthed a silent, screaming prayer: *Frog alert!*

If a hoard of locusts had followed and the Alabama River had turned red, I would not have been surprised that God was using other elements of my world to lead me ever more deeply into the promised land. But couldn't there be a limit? Did we need one more mysterious critter?

Why did a frog come inside this house? I might just as well ask: Where did those figures in Daddy's brain come from? The dustball man, the monkey boy, that guy named Bill who stands beside Daddy's bed at night. Is Bill an angel?

For although I now lived in my daddy's house, where the emanations of his mind seeped out and populated our home, I acknowledged through faith that we also both abided in a supernatural domain — Jesus' creation — where good and evil fight for control of this world. Angels fight devils. God calls sinners to repent, and once a person recognizes Christ as the threshold to eternal life, then the members of that mysterious unity, the Trinity, come and make a home with him or her and bring the peace that passeth understanding. It says so in the Bible. I believe it. Daddy believed it. But when I opened the door to toss the dog a bone, one more unwelcome critter jumped across the threshold to disturb the peace of our home. "It's getting kind of crowded in here!" I shrieked.

"Who are you talking to?" Katie asked, undisturbed by the pitch of my voice.

"I'm talking to God about the frog."

"If you're talking to God, he already knows about the frog," Katie replied with all the sanguine logic of a six-year-old.

"Exactly," I muttered. God already knows about frogs. Why did he let one more unwelcome creature in?

Before I could concoct a theory that attempted to answer what is basically a theological question, Daddy materialized. During the years that Daddy stalked Mother, he learned how to do that. This time he sent his mind up and down the surface of the walls, looking for the door to the bathroom. He still remembers the intention of going to a special place for the function of relieving himself, but he can't recall where it is or find the door. "I need to take your grandfather to the bathroom," I told Katie.

"Why can't he take himself to the bathroom?" she asked, just as Daddy lost control of his bladder and wet himself. It wasn't a very dramatic event. He does it all the time. A small puddle accumulated on the floor at his feet. The room immediately filled with that sour, nutty scent I had first noticed upstairs after we buried Mama. I had not known what it was then. I knew now.

"If we are going to get to bed tonight, I must call for help," I said. I reached for the phone and punched in Guin's number. She lived next door and wasn't afraid of frogs. When she answered, I announced without preamble, "Daddy's messed himself up. I've got Katie with me, and there's a frog in the living room."

"Which problem do you want me to solve?" Guin asked calmly.

"The frog. He's over by the fireplace."

"Leave the back door unlocked. I'll be right there," she said.

She hung up just as I added, "It's a very big frog." Feeling guilty for not having warned her, I said, "Daddy, I'm coming." But he had sent his mind on a time journey, and he couldn't hear me. "Katie, could you go upstairs, turn on the TV, and wait for me?"

"Why can't I stay here with you?"

"Because I'm going to undress your Grandpa, and he wouldn't want you to see him naked."

"He's seen me naked."

I smiled. "You are exactly right, my love. But your grandfather was always a modest man when he remembered who he was, and he wouldn't want you to see him without his britches on, which are about to come off."

Katie giggled. "'Cause he's wet his pants."

"He has indeed. And I've got to clean him up and get him to bed. Then I'll come upstairs to you, and we are going to have warm chocolate milk and cuddle in the big rocker."

"And you'll tell me a story . . ." Her luminous blue eyes held onto mine.

"I will," I promised. "And I'll brush your hair, if you like." She had thick brown hair glossy with captured sunlight.

She nodded, a cooperative, loving child who could understand simple directions and had made many unselfish compromises in her short life in deference to her grandfather's needs. "Good-night, Pa," she said to the statue in front of us. A thin trickle of drool was accumulating in the corner of his mouth.

"He heard you. He just can't answer you right now," I explained.

Katie walked purposefully to the stairs, then hesitated. "Will it take long?" It was dark at the top of the stairs, and she looked longingly at me. I walked over and flipped the switch that lit the upstairs hallway.

What did time feel like to her? I looked at Daddy's face: *Where was he? What was time to him?* I checked the hour on the kitchen clock. It was seven-thirty. I had never timed how long it took me to strip Dad, wash him down, and redress him. How many minutes would it be exactly?

Not knowing the answer, I made up one. "Be there in twenty minutes," I said. *When an Alzheimer's patient makes up an answer, doctors call
it a symptom of the disease and assign it a fancy name: confabulation.*

Katie nodded as if we had made a business deal. I confirmed that
the back door was unlocked so Guin could get in, and then, pretending the frog was not last seen behind the chair I needed to pass, I
cooed, "Come, Jerry."

He didn't respond at all. He looked the way he used to when we
all thought he had a hearing problem. He could actually hear pretty
well, however, when his mind was present. He was holding the remote control to the TV again. I took his hand and stroked the back of
it till the physical pressure snagged a part of his attention. Suddenly
he was present. He looked at me and smiled. "Where have you been?"
he asked.

My jaw dropped. He hadn't spoken to me in a couple of days.

"I've been around," I said.

"I'm glad to see you. I've missed you. Did you get any good writing
done today?"

"I've missed you, too." I said truthfully. I didn't answer his other
question, for I was not writing very much, except to scribble snippets
of dialogue on little pieces of paper and then lose them. As far as my
writing was concerned, I felt like I was in some unnamed body of water, caught in a riptide that was pulling me farther and farther away
from the shore.

"I was about to collect the rent," Daddy said plainly. "You want to
come with me?"

He thought we were in his old apartment building on Alabama
Street again. I had swept the foyer and gone with him to collect the
rent every first of the month. Those were good days, and, strangely, I
was happy for him to be there. "I was hoping you'd ask," I replied.

"Which apartment shall we go to first?" he asked.

"That one," I said, pointing behind him to the big room where he
slept now. He couldn't manage stairs anymore. "Let's go there."

His body came to life, and his mind attempted to send him where
I asked that we go. He smiled, and there was a hole where a tooth had

been that we could not replace. Daddy can't follow the instructions of a dentist, and I won't allow them to put him to sleep. *Every time you put an Alzheimer's patient to sleep, he doesn't wake up with as much of himself as was there before he went under.*

We walked slowly, as if meandering through a garden where blossoms elicited our appreciation. When we were finally in the laundry room next to his room, the sight of the washing machine triggered a self-conscious response. "I'm dirty," he declared.

"You are right, but it's okay. I'll help you get cleaned up," I said.

"You've always been a hard worker," he approved.

"That's me," I affirmed.

Eventually we reached the back room. I stripped Daddy systematically, breathing Julie Ann's prayer: *God, make my hands go where they don't want to go.*

As soon as he was bare-assed, I wrapped one of the towel-skirts around him, pressing the Velcro ends together. He was cooperating enough so that I could lead him to the back bathroom, get him into the shower stall, and wash him, then pat him dry. Upstairs, I could hear my niece moving around. Patient. Very patient for a six-year-old.

The knowledge of her up there made me want to hurry. Daddy immediately sensed the shift in my tempo and grew nervous. Anxiety made him stumble, slowed him down. I willed myself not to hurry. We both sighed. I got him dressed in his night-time outfit, led him to his bed. Sat him down. Picked up his legs, playing the same baby game that had killed my mother.

Daddy grew stiff, and I had to arrange him. When he was finally prone, he held his head up as if there were a pillow under it. There wasn't. I placed a pillow beneath his head and, putting my hand on his forehead, pressed gently down. His eyes registered confusion, as if I were committing an act of aggression against him. I pressed my cheek against his and whispered, "I love you. Say your prayers and go to sleep."

"Yes, Mama."

"Now I lay me down to sleep," I prompted. His eyes roamed the room and finally found mine.

"Now I lay me down to sleep," I repeated.

"I pray the Lord my soul to keep," he replied.

"Amen," I said. "Now sleep in peace."

Tonight I couldn't wait for him to adjust to the bed. I tucked him in and then gripped his foot. My heart uttered a mercy prayer: *Lord, help me to hear him if he needs me.*

"I'm just in the other room. The baby monitor is on. If you need me, call out. I'll hear you." He didn't know what I was saying, but I needed to say it. Would I hear him? *God, don't let him be alone and afraid.*

He squeezed his eyes shut fast, as if he were blanking out visions he couldn't stand, and his hands gripped the edge of the covers as if he were in a lifeboat, holding onto the sides. I switched on a table lamp and left him, turning in the doorway that led to the laundry room to take a last look. Head suddenly down, mouth open, he began inhaling great draughts of air. Within minutes, he would be snoring. I grabbed a dirty towel off the floor of the laundry room to wipe up the urine in the kitchen, but Guin had already done that. She had left me a note: "Big frog gone. Get some sleep. Call anytime. You are not alone." Guin's faithfulness to my family had redefined friendship. So many words had been redefined since Daddy got sick: *Love, memory, time, father, gratitude.*

"Thank you, God," I whispered, dropping the towel as I headed upstairs to my niece. I stopped in the bathroom to wash my hands once more with disinfectant soap, then found our little girl sitting in the rocker, wearing her nightshirt.

"I don't want to take a bath tonight," she announced as soon as I came in. She had brushed her own hair and plaited it down the back. Otherwise, it got all tangled up in her sleep.

"Have you brushed your teeth?" I asked gently. I had taken much longer than twenty minutes.

"I do that after I have my chocolate milk," she replied woodenly, staring ahead. Her feelings were hurt because I had taken so long.

"Are you ready for that now?" I asked.

Katie nodded, turning. "You promised to tell me a story."

I went to the small refrigerator, poured a cup of chocolate milk, and zapped it in the microwave. Katie made a place for me beside her in the rocker. After I joined her, she took the milk and said, "Now, rock!" My foot commenced the motion that mothers have always known.

"Story," she demanded next.

"There once was a little girl named Katie," I began.

"Good." She liked stories that were about heroines named after her.

"And this little girl loved blueberries."

"I love blueberries."

"And she had a blueberry bush that was big and fat with lots of green berries on it."

"Like ours," she said, snuggling against my chest.

"Yes, like ours. And every day she went outside to the bush to see if the berries were getting ripe . . ."

"Because she loved blueberries. I love blueberries. And blackberries."

"I know you do. But the berries kept staying green."

"So she prayed that God would turn them blue," Katie whispered, as if telling me a secret.

"Yes, she prayed that God would make them ripe and turn them blue. The sun came up and shined and shined, creating the miracle of daylight."

"And that was three days," Katie counted.

"And on the fourth day, the berries at the top of the bush began to turn pink . . ."

"And she ate one."

"She ate one very sour pink berry."

"And it turned her pink."

"How did you know?" I asked in mock surprise.

"You've told me this story before. I like this story," Katie confided.

"And her mother gave her some milk and said, 'Don't eat the berries till they're blue.'"

"But the next day, they were only a darker pink."

"And she ate another one."

"And it turned her dark pink . . ."

Katie smiled, her skin translucent and holy. "Can we make some more blueberry jelly?"

"I imagine we can," I said.

"But then one day she woke up, and the bush was more blue than any other color — so blue that you could barely see the green leaves. And she got a bowl and began to pick the berries, but she didn't eat any because she had this idea that she would give some to everyone in her family, and let them turn blue, and she would laugh."

"But it didn't work like that," Katie explained.

"No," I said.

"Because blueberries are supposed to be blue. They won't make you sick or turn you colors," Katie continued.

"That's right. And then her mother told her that poem about the seasons."

Katie nudged me. I settled back deeply into the chair and let Scripture do the work appointed for it.

"To everything there is a season, a time for every purpose under heaven. A time to be born, and a time to die."

"Grandmother died because it was time," Katie said suddenly, her mind taking a sharp turn.

"That's right," I agreed. I took a deep breath and rocked. "A time to plant, and a time to pluck what is planted."

"When the blueberries are blue."

"The end," I said.

"I like that story," she said. "And I like the story about the brother and sister, the one where the brother takes all his money and goes off to town and spends it all until he has to eat with the pigs. And he comes back home, and his sister gets mad 'cause her Daddy gives that bad boy a big welcome-home party, but he never gave her a party, and she'd been good the whole time."

"I like that one too. Your granddaddy used to tell that story every time he got the chance. Your granddaddy used to preach," I said.

"That daddy should have given the good girl who stayed at home a party without her asking," Katie replied sleepily.

"She was supposed to ask. He told her that everything he had was hers, that all she had to do was ask for it. She had to remember that. That was the lesson she learned."

"Do you think she asked for a party?" Katie wondered drowsily.

"Maybe more than one," I said.

"Is that a true story?"

"Yes," I said. "That last story is from the Bible. It's 'The Prodigal Son,' and it's a completely trustworthy story. It tells the truth about how much God loves us. I changed it a little bit — I gave the boy who left home a good sister instead of a good brother — but it's still the same story. The stories in the Bible teach us about God's love when we read them, or tell them, or . . ."

"Hear them," Katie whispered.

"That's right. God likes to hear our stories too. That's why he wants us to pray — to talk to him. Our prayers are the true stories of our lives that we tell to him. Are you ready to say your prayers?"

"You," she said, eyelids fluttering, breathing slowing to that pace that allows the good dreams to come, and when they do, they bring meaning and hope to waking life.

"Now I lay you down to sleep," I began for the second time that night. "I pray the Lord your soul to keep."

Katie relaxed in my arms, and I held her.

From the Family Album . . .

Resurrection

He sleeps too much, curled up in his bed like a human question mark.

I wander in and out of his room, perching temporarily on the side of his bed, rubbing his back, kissing his bewhiskered face, and beseeching him to rouse. Five attempts get me nowhere. The offer of freshly brewed coffee does not work. I pace. I pray. I go back to the kitchen to unload the dishwasher, pondering the nature of my daddy's illness and the course it is taking.

Three weeks ago we found him unconscious on the floor. By ambulance we took him to the hospital. While the nurse and I were appraising him in his semiconscious state, his clothes soiled, bruises surfacing on his face from having landed on it when he fell, and she was asking me if I wanted extraordinary measures employed to keep him alive, I replied, "This man can get up and walk out of here anytime he wants."

I was the only person who thought that ending possible. Everyone else was predicting the end of his life. I stood in front of Daddy, immobile in his hospital bed, and I asked, "Are you ready to go home?"

He got right up. People backed away from the mystery of his return to life by simply being offered the refuge of home. Following hospital procedure, we negotiated the wheelchair. Once we were outside by the car, I had to help him get up. Trying to rise, he lost his balance and grabbed hold of my left breast for support. When he wouldn't let go, strangers gawked. I was embarrassed and amused by the ridiculousness of our position, but instead of crying, I laughed. My daddy was present, in his way, and I was glad.

I brought my old man home, but he wasn't the same as before this most recent fall in a series of tumbles. Before this last ambulance ride . . . Before . . . My life and care of him involve a continual comparison of his very fluid symptoms of today with what they seemed like yesterday. I do the job of gauging the slippage of his faculties, his physical abilities, his reasoning, which sometimes boils down to whether he can sit on a commode or not. He is now mostly docile, but that cooperation has been signaling a private message to me too, like a faint but decipherable code that vibrates between us. This morning I think he's been in the bed too long. One more time, I think he could get up if he only wanted to.

"Jerry Simpkins," I address him formally, switching tactics.

"You've been playing possum. It's time you got your lazy, skinny butt out of that bed."

The muffled voice comes from under the covers. He can talk today. "I'm a lot of trouble," he says. It is an apology.

My voice firm, I reply, "You're more trouble to me in the bed. Get up and let me give you a shave. Besides, no matter what shape you're in, I want you with me. Come enjoy what you can of the day."

He grins, then chuckles. I'd like to think he feels loved, because he is.

"I knew you were in there," I said, leaning over to kiss him on the cheek. "I think your depression is back. You're going to have to fight the desire to sleep, or the bed will take you." I offer the hot coffee again. This time it is accepted.

An hour later he is bathed and dressed, and we are headed to Hardee's for breakfast biscuits. He falls asleep in the car before he can eat his, but I get him moving again and inside the house. Then he eats his two sausage biscuits before Patty Kate comes by to see how he is doing. "He looks good," she says. "He must be having a good day."

"He is," I reply, and then I add what I have learned with my daddy is the truth, "Every day is a good day."

18

Party Girl

I woke up one morning feeling like I wanted a party. I needed party supplies: toilet paper, napkins, paper towels, detergent, Clorox, and chocolate.

I had the money. I had the time. I had a car. But I had my Daddy. I still wanted a party! I wanted to go to K-mart!

I took an appraising look at him. He was standing and sitting today. He had just gone to the bathroom. That could hold him an hour. K-mart wasn't far from here, just across town in the parallel universe where people who are considered not crazy meet to shop. *God, can we please go to K-mart?*

As if reading my mind, Daddy said, "I want to go for a ride."

"Me, too. Where do you want to go?" I asked.

"Anywhere you want to go," he answered agreeably.

"K-mart?" I asked.

"Okay, Grandmama."

I was grandmother today. So be it. "Let's go," I said, as I blocked Daddy's view of the doorknob, because if he ever gets a-hold of one, he won't let go.

Safely past the temptation of a round, shiny object, we were out the front door, where the sun was shining. Birds were singing.

I suddenly remembered something important: Like God, Beauty is. I remembered that beauty arises from symmetry. Usually this orderly arrangement of the parts of a whole produces the effect of beauty. As I looked at my father, my understanding of beauty suddenly expanded to encompass his chaos and beauty's dependence upon it for definition. Although opposites, each has inherent in it the power to break the human heart.

While holding the car door open for Daddy, I imagined falling on my face in the dirt and giving thanks to God for beauty and for my daddy, who had, in this very moment, helped me experience the knowledge of God's beauty differently. Worshipping God in my spirit while still performing physical work is a new benefit of living in this promised land.

I now abide in a variety of realities, moving in and out of them as fluidly as Daddy's hallucinations come and go. I praised God for this flexibility of my mind to move in concert with Daddy's, sending an unspoken prayer that though I can and do adapt to chaos, I preferred not to embody it myself. As this felt like a betrayal of my dear daddy, I sent an apology his way, and he smiled at me. I was glad to be alive.

I psyched myself up to talk Daddy into getting in the car. But a miracle happened, and I didn't even ask for it. Daddy just got in the car. *Thank you, Jesus.*

Oh, we had the best time driving to K-mart. Out of joy I was singing in my heart on my way to pick up party supplies, and suddenly Daddy began to sing the same song playing inside of me. We sang a duet: *Blessed assurance, Jesus is mine! O, what a foretaste of glory divine. Heir of salvation, purchase of God, born of his Spirit, washed in his blood. This is my story, this is my song, praising my Savior all the day long. This is my story, this is my song, praising my Savior all the day long.*

I had no rational explanation for praising God while Daddy was in this kind of shape. I knew only that I could not quench the gratitude I felt for my daddy beside me — and in that moment, Daddy even sounded like his old self. How could I make this happen again? I tabled my question as I turned into K-mart's parking lot. Daddy fumbled with the door, and I helped him open it. Then we were standing together outside in a public place, and his pants were not wet. *Glory to God.*

He took my hand. "Where are we going, Mother?"

K-mart looked golden, shining in the morning dew, an oasis of riches. They had toilet paper and soap in there. As Daddy and I navigated the traffic, I stole a look at him. He was walking, walking, head up — sort of. The doors were the sliding electric kind — not a doorknob on them! They opened for us — a mysterious phenomenon that I did not try to explain to Daddy, who would have liked to repeat this pleasure.

I retrieved a shopping cart and placed Dad's hands upon it. "Thataway."

Using the cart as a walker, he sprinted fleet-of-foot while I pretended I was on Supermarket Sweep. Up and down the aisles we went very fast, with Daddy setting a fast, erratic pace. Sometimes his tempo drove me crazy, but today I thought it was hilarious. Laughing, I piled the buggy high with pure luxury items. We would have Kleenex again. Paper plates. I stacked five hundred coffee filters on top. *God, you are merciful.* Ohhhhh, they had candy here! Chocolate Hershey bars. I moaned as if I were being reunited with an old, passionate lover who could really kiss. Daddy and I grinned over the Hershey bars, and I said, "Party time!"

We spent twenty whole minutes in paradise and then proceeded to the checkout, where we only had to wait behind one buggy — another miracle. Two women belonged to it, and they were laughing and talking in a British accent. Their voices brought back Wordsworth's view of daily life with his sister Dorothy, who went crazy on him: *For I have learned to look on nature, not as in the hour of thoughtless youth; but hearing oftentimes the still, sad music of humanity.*

"Promise you'll kill me if I ever get very sick," one of the British ladies asked her friend.

"I'll murder you straightaway," her companion promised politely.

"Even if you have to go to jail?"

"Anything for you, dear."

"How will you do it?"

"Poison. Gun." The friend shrugged nonchalantly. "Do you have a preference?"

"Give me a strong sleeping pill. Then drown me in a bathtub.

There's a good chance you could get away with murder that way. It really could look like an accident, don't you think?"

"Brilliant. And of course, you will do the same for me?"

I couldn't see their faces, but I watched Delia, the cashier, who wore a practiced blank expression. Should either of these two women become suddenly dead in the near future and their movements get backtracked by a detective to K-mart, Delia was ready to say, *I didn't hear nothing. I don't even remember those two foreigners in my checkout line. I wait on a million customers a day. How'm I s'posed to remember them?*

"Who are they?" Daddy asked, tension gathering in his face.

"The Kervorkian sisters," I replied. "We don't know them."

"Somebody has died. Do we need to go to the funeral?"

"Not yet," I said, as the two women left, laughing.

We were checked out efficiently, and I pushed our loaded buggy to the car. I opened the passenger door for Daddy and said, "Sit." It sounded like I was ordering him around, but long, polite sentences troubled Daddy. I began to amend my sentence patterns and word choices right after I said to him one time, "Will you please stand up?" and he replied, quite sensibly, "Stand up to what?"

"Sit in the car," I repeated, as he gripped the door handle and pushed on it. I didn't rush him. He lives in a different time zone. I speedily unloaded the buggy, putting all of the sacks in the trunk except for the party supplies, which I placed within arm's reach on the back seat. But when I was finished, Daddy was still standing. "Get inside the car. Party time."

Knowing he was supposed to do something but unsure what, Daddy simply folded up in front of me, balancing on the running board of the car. People in the store's parking lot stopped in their tracks, sacks ready to be tossed aside if they concluded from the drama unfolding that the old man being bossed around needed rescuing from me. Seeing their concern, I waved cheerily and said, "It's all right. He's just crazy."

They didn't believe me. I decided that I had better get Daddy in the car before someone called the cops on me and accused me of elder abuse, so I leaned over and barked in a short command that my Alzheimer-ridden Daddy might be able to process and that passing strangers concluded was my shrewish need to dominate an old man, "Get in the car."

"I am in the car," he said, looking up at me. He thought I was playing with him, and he began to giggle.

His laughter was contagious, and I might have stopped a moment, as I have many times, to explode in hysterics over the ridiculousness of our situation if I hadn't had so many witnesses who might have construed my laughter as a cold-hearted glee gained from torturing a senior citizen who was scared enough of me to cower at my feet.

"You are not in the car. You are stuck on the running board. Your feet are still on the pavement," I explained, as a man Daddy's age returned his shopping cart to the corral and called to me, his voice rife with suspicion, "Is everything okay over there?"

"We're just fine," I said. Lips splitting from the strain of smiling, I reached down, grabbed Daddy by his pants' waistband, and hoisted him into the car. Daddy fell over on the front seat laughing.

The other man gave me the evil eye, and I hurried around to the driver's side, lifting Daddy's head so that I could wedge in behind the wheel. "Please sit up," I begged tiredly.

Daddy could no longer hear me. So I levered him upright, fastened his seat belt, and wiped the drool from his mouth. "Have you had a good outing?" I asked brightly, backing out of our parking space. My heart was racing. A muscle was strained in my neck, and I felt my regular headache begin there. The euphoria of our trip to paradise had passed. Daddy's chin drifted to his chest, and like a child who has played too hard, he suddenly fell asleep.

I drove the long way home, down Cobbs Ford Road, past the Christmas-tree farm where early-bird shoppers were already buying their trees. Thinking that the city had probably already put out the holiday decorations, I snuck up on Main Street from the other side. I turned into the parking lot of the city's park. The peppermint bough was in place. Mr. and Mrs. Claus were already standing with the elves positioned around them. The wishing well was lit. It was picturesque. I have a terrible appetite for the picturesque, and in that moment I submitted to that craving.

I turned off the engine, and as soon as I did, Daddy woke up. Saliva pooled in the corner of his mouth, and I daubed at it with one of the paper napkins I kept handy for that job. From the back seat I drew forth the sack with the Hershey bars in it and a six-pack of juice boxes. "Let's have our party now," I invited.

His consciousness traveled the circumference of the walking trail in the park, a quarter mile, and then returned like a scavenger that is searching for clues, facts, meaning. It is the impulse that never quits. He strained to find me in the car, his one good eye peering at me curiously.

"You know me," I coaxed. "We are in the park."

I broke the Hershey bar into bite-size squares and laid them on a napkin on the seat between us. "Chocolate," I offered, but his nap had made him groggy. He stared off into space. I felt so often like I was talking to myself. It was a strange phenomenon, to be so close to someone else and still be so alone. Wordsworth had understood this moment: *If I should be where I no more can hear thy voice, nor catch from thy wild eyes these gleams of past existence — wilt thou then forget that on the banks of this delightful stream we stood together?*

Would I ever forget this moment in time with Daddy, when we were so alone and even the tensions of authority and rebellion had been made moot by the thief that had robbed him of the knowledge of who he was and who I am? Picking up a chocolate square, I touched it to his lips, and he automatically opened his mouth. When his lips parted, I slid the tender candy into his mouth as if it were a communion wafer and rested it on his tongue. I waited a minute or so for the chocolate to dissolve. Then I placed the thin straw of the juice box between his lips. I squeezed the box, pumping liquid through the straw. He gagged.

"I'm so sorry," I said, mopping up juice and chocolate drool.

His head bobbed. When his chin bounced off his chest, the residue of chocolate fell out of his mouth, and I caught it with the napkin.

"The party's over," I said. "I'll take you home."

We made the five-minute drive home in a silence that didn't hum with shared thoughts or songs. It was a still silence. The images of the town flew by. There were people headed out to play golf, people toting Christmas trees on the roofs of their cars, people going to The Smoke House for barbecue. Did they remember that this day was a gift, every minute precious — every fleeting moment a memory in the making?

At home, another car was in the driveway. Mary Ellen was sitting on the front porch, holding a coffee cup. She held up the cup as part greeting, part inquiry: Was she welcome? I responded to the unspoken question.

"I'm glad to see you. How are you?" I asked.

Her eyes refused to lie. "Good," she declared firmly. She looked beautiful. Her hair was lighter, with some red in it. Her enormous hazel eyes were clear and filled with intelligence but also the shadows of pain outlived but not forgotten.

"We've been to K-mart. That's just chocolate on Daddy's shirt. Not blood. Happy birthday, by the way . . ."

"Thanks," she said. "Is he asleep?"

I nodded, opening the trunk of the car. She put her cup down and rose. There was a new strength that I had not seen in her before. "I'll help you," she offered, reaching for some sacks.

Suddenly I couldn't lift a single bag. She recognized immediately the extent of my fatigue.

"Sit down," she directed. "I'll do this."

Mary Ellen carried in four bags at one time and returned with a cup of coffee for me.

"Daddy," I said. Sometimes it's the only word left in me. Often my prayers are reduced to this one word, and I don't know if I'm calling on God or asking God to see about Daddy.

"He's asleep, and he's all right. Drink your coffee."

Could I lift the cup?

How had I driven to the store and back with this much fatigue in me, waiting on the opportunity to announce itself in this sudden immobility just because my sister had come home? Mary Ellen pretended that she didn't see how tired I was. She finished unloading the car.

When the trunk was empty, she left the lid up, because closing it might wake Daddy. Then she rejoined me on the porch. I felt a new energy pulsing from her.

"You brought home everything we could need. Mother was like that. She believed in keeping the house stocked."

"I saw two women at K-mart today," I told her. "They were discussing killing each other if assigned a catastrophic illness that puts too great a burden on others."

Mary Ellen nodded knowingly, considering the problem to be solved. "I'd use a pillow," she mused. "Place it over the face of the sick person and say, 'Talk to the pillow.'"

"*Pillow Talk.*" I laughed at the idea of Doris Day performing euthanasia. "Would you ever do it?"

"No," she said flatly. "Neither would you. You always want to see the end of the story."

I smiled. "That's one reason," I agreed. It is very sweet to be understood.

Mary Ellen looked off toward what had once been her own house. "I can hear my tulips calling me sometimes," she confessed suddenly. "I think I might go down there and dig up my bulbs. Do you want to help me?"

"That would be stealing," I said.

"If I can hear them, they're still mine," she asserted, eyes glinting with amusement.

I laughed, and she did too. "I'm better now," she said.

"I can see that."

Mary Ellen was fresh with a new fearlessness, and there was power in her. She had been separated from the family in a way that had allowed for this independence — only she wanted to spend her strength on the family whose needs were in many ways not good for her. The world uses words like "codependent," "dysfunctional," and "crazy" to describe us both. Those words don't tell the whole truth. We simply loved each other to the point of being ready to die while expressing that love.

Mary Ellen kept her eyes focused on Daddy, willing him to sleep in peace. Her mind flew to him and circled overhead, patrolling the universe for darts from the enemy that might try to steal him away before the day that had been appointed for his release. I let her pull the sentry duty.

"Daddy is going to die soon," she predicted suddenly.

"Yes. He's having trouble swallowing," I said. "Aunt Eileen said when that begins to happen, we're coming to the end."

"Do the other girls know?"

"Probably," I said. "I think before he got sick, he was the smartest man I've ever known. But during his illness, I've never been prouder of him in my whole life. I have probably adored Daddy too much."

"That's because he's still pretty close to being perfect," Mary Ellen said, forgiving him of accusing her son falsely, of hurting her. Forgiveness brought peace.

We tossed the remains of our coffee on the ground as a silent pact between us and rose together to go and get Daddy from the car. I climbed in through the driver's side to push. At the passenger door, Mary Ellen lifted his legs down. Then, taking his hands, she pulled him up.

He had wet his pants, and chocolate drool still dripped from his mouth. His nose leaked. Standing in front of Daddy, Mary Ellen wiped his nose and mouth and held him till he got his bearings. He was speechless again. She smiled at him. "Hello, Gorgeous. Anybody home?"

He concentrated on the question, unable to answer it. She took his hands again and led him to the house that he once upon a time had built from the ground up. I moved quickly to open the front door and hide the doorknob with my body. When my sister passed me, leading our Daddy into the only sanctuary we could provide, she whispered, "Isn't he the most beautiful man you've ever seen?"

An Angel's Kiss

In the carefully modulated tones adopted for his profession, my father's psychiatrist turns and says to me, "You know by now that you have a vocation for this kind of nursing, don't you?"

I am so stunned to be addressed personally that it takes me a couple of seconds before I can nod yes.

There have been other surprises with the psychiatrist. The initial steps undertaken to diagnose Alzheimer's surprised me, for it was accomplished only through the process of elimination. Since then, I have been surprised that there was no search for real meaning in conversations with Daddy. There was never any real attempt to figure out the relevance or the nature of his hallucinations. There was no interest in his dream life, no serious acknowledgment of either his desire or his need for company other than his daughters. From the first time I took Daddy to the psychiatrist, there was only one consistent, surprising response to his mental problems: chemicals.

I came to hate the mention of medicine for what ailed my daddy; but, like people with cancer who resort to the torture of chemo and radiation treatment, I kept trying, attempting to find some kind of antidote for Daddy's condition, only to determine in the long run that what ailed him was a kind of accelerated aging process happening mostly in his brain. His body's still in pretty good shape, but his mind's a mess.

The state of his mind is the reason for this visit. The psychiatrist has a litany of questions he asks Daddy when we come in for our assessment. They are diagnostic questions disguised as conversation. I understand his intent, but I still don't like the deceit of it.

When Dr. Haldol says, "I like your shirt, Jerry," I know that he is trying to make a personal connection that will lead to the tricky litany: How are you? Are they feeding you enough? Are you sleeping okay? What is today, Jerry? Is it summertime? Christmastime?

The problem with being a witness to this kind of verbal diagnosis and subterfuge is that I don't trust Dr. Haldol when he says things to me like, "You know you have a vocation for this kind of nursing, don't you?" I think he might have some ulterior motive for saying it. So I don't answer him — don't tell him the truth. It feels like self-defense when I don't admit what I know: "I think in symbols and that helps me manage a person suffering from dementia."

I can move in and out of my daddy's imagined worlds. When he described the characters that inhabit his interior worlds, I recognized immediately that the small man wearing the black cap and cape, the one who holds his forearm up to his eyes, is a projection of my daddy hiding himself from us the best he can.

Other reported hallucinations, like the rolling dustball that speaks and the crew that plays dominoes, reveal different aspects of his nature — his humility and his longing for intimate company.

"Are you pacing yourself?" Dr. Haldol asks now, sympathetically.

I censor myself again. I do not say, "What do you mean, am I pacing myself? I don't control the pace. Daddy's disease dictates it. Don't try to burden me with a sense that I have control over it."

I have no control. I have only love. I still tell Daddy all the time how much I love him, sometimes nervously, sometimes longingly, sometimes because it feels like the last time he might hear me. And when he complains, I listen. When he says that the cabinet doors make too much noise when I close them, I don't tell him he's crazy. I put new felt door-stoppers on them to absorb the sound. And I buy all of his linens in a soothing blue because some print designs scare him, and I change his bed every time it needs it, and I mop his room every day, and I pray for him unceasingly.

I don't tell the psychiatrist that I pray. We don't talk about God, the same way we don't talk about what's going on in my daddy's dream world or in mine. Not long ago, I had a tantalizing dream about my daddy. I hold onto the dream, turning it over and over in my mind. I dreamed this: I was standing behind the house where my parents lived, and a small, gnome-like man walked through the wall and into the basement. Then a celestial being, probably an angel, appeared beside me with a message that made perfect sense: "He was born that way, and there is nothing you can do about it."

I believed him and immediately laid down to rest in the green grass beside the creek that runs behind my parents' home. Then the angel leaned over and kissed my lips, and his mouth was like rose petals.

That was the dream. I know that it is like one of my daddy's hallucinations, only I still retain citizenship in the world called normal, so I am allowed to ascribe a subjective meaning to it, which I do freely without demanding that anyone else agree with my interpretation.

I don't need anyone in a position of authority to sanctify my idea of meaning anymore. I have learned that she who survives has earned the right to consider herself right. Wrong is being unable to manage; surviving — thriving, even — means you're right.

And that means when the psychiatrist tells me that I have a vocation for nursing mental patients, I receive the compliment without pursuing the question of whether his conversation is double-edged, as it is with the small talk he makes with my daddy, or whether he is simply uttering a sentence he thinks is true.

I think it is true, but I think I have a vocation for this because I believe in the importance of finding meaning in chaos and giving love without limits, and I don't think psychiatry deals with meaning when the sick person has Alzheimer's, and any time I ever mention love, Dr. Haldol keeps his face blank.

There is love, however, and love is more than the effect of behaviors modified by parents and tradition or a state produced by chemicals. Love is the power that makes endurance possible in whatever circumstances a person finds herself living or dreaming or asking questions about both. Love comes from God the Father, who is real.

I believe in God.

I believe in asking questions that may have answers as vaporous as the description of a hallucination.

I believe in telling the truth when I can, no matter how crazy it might make me look to others.

I believe in love and dreams and lying down in green pastures and receiving and remembering an angel's kiss that felt like rose petals.

19

God Is Love

I am awakened by the implanted revelation that Daddy needs me.
I pick up my eyeglasses, which need to be changed. My vision is
deteriorating, or so it seems to me, but no one has confirmed my diagnosis. I don't have a way to go to the eye doctor or any other kind of
doctor. I haven't been in three years. The piano hasn't been tuned in
five.

In the shadows of early morning, I move as Mother did before me
to the stairs, where I stand and listen for Daddy.

I do not hear him. Do I imagine his need of me? Is God speaking?
Is it only one of the interior voices inside my own head trying to get
itself born in a story? I no longer worry about why the many selves of
personhood do not coalesce into one perfect self. I know only one
thing: I trust God's love and the expression of it. "Jesus," I testify.

The loneliness of Daddy's spirit speaks into the deep recesses of
my soul, and I whisper, "I'm on my way," though Daddy has not called
out, and when I speak, he does not answer me.

Down the stairs I go, my bones creaking, and I wonder if at forty-
four I have some disease that could possibly be cured if I had a good
doctor. I let go of the question. The answer is irrelevant. I will live as
long as I am supposed to live, and then I will die.

I find my Daddy.

He is standing in the kitchen, behind the stairs, and he, quite simply, has exploded. His body is covered in urine and excrement, and he

can't figure out what to do about it. He is immobilized, a statue. He is drooling.

"Help me, God." I repeat my prayer. I fall to my knees, and in faith that I will last long enough to do the work, my hands go where they do not want to be. I begin stripping my beautiful daddy. It is not an easy job to undress a man who cannot follow directions as well as a child. This is not a baby's game.

I will not go into the details of the clean-up. I will tell only the important part of the story.

Just as I felt my daddy's presence and his need of me before I descended the stairs, I felt the presence of Love Itself — God — in the room while I tended my sick daddy. As the Fount of Love kept me company in the daylight, so Love was present in the darkness too.

Strength not my own moved my body.

Strength not my own moved my daddy.

Once the clothes were in a soiled puddle on the floor, I led my naked, trusting daddy by the hand to the bathroom. We walked slowly, without a blanket or towel to wrap around him. Suddenly we were confronted by the image of ourselves in the only mirror left in the living room: the pink-tinted mirror. I stopped in that sudden moment of recognition of a truth that had been waiting to get born. My daddy was bent over at the waist, shrunken from age and illness. His reflection felt like that previously unrecognizable child I had once seen in the mirror of my dream years ago. "I don't care how this looks. God is in control," I vowed to the reflection.

Strength to persevere grew out of this proclamation. That is a fact.

The man who had preached the gospel faithfully stood abjectly, obedient to my leading. I led Daddy to the walk-in shower stall. After testing the water, I began at the top of his head and worked my way down, scrubbing, rinsing, scrubbing, rinsing, checking the crevices of his body for residue of waste and suds that might cause him to have a latent rash.

My beautiful daddy. Oh, I crooned words of praise for my daddy in his dilapidated state of confusion, and the sound of my voice was not an imitation of love that good girls admit in infantile crushes over their first hero; my voice was a prayer of praise and beseechment, a mercy prayer that wrought results and peace and kept me in company with the Presence of Love.

When Daddy was clean and dressed again, only two hours had passed, and I put him back to bed, and he was asleep before he lay down. I lifted his legs, and covered him, and kissed his face, and whispered in his ear that I was never far away. Only then did the muscles in his face grow slack, because his spirit knows the sound of my voice even if his brain no longer registers the meaning of the words. He trusts me with his life. *3*

Then I sat in the corner chair during that long good night until the sun came up, and I thanked God for the expression of his love that can even look like death. *go to 195*

Daddy, I knew you were leaving the day the refrigerator stopped working again. I went and got the vacuum cleaner and used it like we had before, but nothing happened. When the motor didn't kick in, and all the cups of ice cream and yogurt that we kept stocked for you melted, I knew you were going to leave soon. I didn't try to save any of the special foods we had bought for you. I let them go to waste, like expensive oil poured on your feet, anointing you in a way that was more emotional than reasonable.

And for nine days at least your body hesitated, your mind coming and going as you waited for Julie Ann to come from Memphis. All of us took our turns beside you in the time of your leavetaking, when loving you was not a caregiving duty — it was our identity and unexpectedly, at times, our joy.

By the way, I took Katie shoe-shopping the day that Hospice came in and urged us to tell you that it was all right to go on. I took our little girl shoe-shopping, and I bought her six pairs of new shoes because I wanted her to associate death with going places — different kinds of exciting places, where a girl needs all kinds of footgear for traveling.

Katie retained that faithful habit of coming to tell you good night every night until the end. She would begin singing "Silent Night," and then the rest of us would harmonize with her small lead voice, deferring to the innocence and hope of a lullaby that says farewell and hello in the way that only the gospel can.

We did not try to keep her from you, or keep you from anyone who wanted to say good-bye. Matthew and Shan came. Jerrod. Steve. Lola Leigh and Jon.

From greater distances, friends murmured farewell in their way. Spirit-led prayers infiltrated the deep silence of this extended good-bye. Esther prayed. Eileen phoned. Uncle Joe-Joe and Marlene called too. Jody and Rhonda and Jan and Ben stayed close.

My turn came for that bedside conversation — to tell you good-bye — and I told the truth as I understood it and was able to give voice to it: I have adored you, and I always will. You look like you're dying, but the truth is, I think your soul is trying to get born. Go be with a love that is greater than mine.

Later that night, Daddy went looking for Mother. He found her with God.

On the day we buried Daddy, I dressed up that girl who looks like me, can pretend to be me, and answers when someone says my name. She put on a new black-and-blue pantsuit that was three sizes smaller than the last pantsuit she bought before her daddy's illness stopped her from needing clothes that were presentable.

One by one, family members stopped by and whispered words of condolence in her ear. Eventually all of the mourners who were scheduled to caravan across the Alabama River together were present, and they were dressed for church.

At the funeral home, the cars were parked in the lanes designated by the mortician, and then the family went in the side entrance that people who have attended a number of funerals know to take because it is near the bathroom, the water fountain, and the first available box of Kleenex. The parlor where Jerry's casket rested was just to the right, and she stopped with the other girls who looked like his daughters, and they tallied how many people had come by to sign the visitors' book.

A lot.

There was an hour to kill before formal visitation commenced, and the girl who answered to my name retreated more and more so that finally there was only the barest form of life in her, but that spark was enough to continue to make polite conversation and elicit nervous, awkward praise from people who came to pay their respects and didn't know what else to say, so they said, "You're the picture of strength."

Okay, she thought. Praise, condemnation — it was all the same to her now. All she wanted was to get through the funeral, then go home and sleep or die, whichever felt right.

Hymns were played softly on an organ.

Okay. Hymns were okay.

Hands were shaken. Cheeks kissed. She didn't dare look at the coffin and see Jerry's face, until finally she remembered that Mama hadn't looked like herself, and it had been a great relief to realize that her mama wasn't there in that box, and so she looked, but he was her daddy after all.

Okay. Daddy died. Better to face the truth. She knew that. It had been a long time since she could afford the luxury of not facing the truth.

"Jerry was a good friend to me," a stranger said.

"And to me," she replied for me. *Good girl.*

"You girls were blessed."

"We were," she replied, sounding just the way she wanted to sound. In control, but not cold. People had said she was cold at her mother's funeral because she hadn't cried. She knew better. Crying was contagious. If she had started crying, then all her sisters would have cried, and they would have been a mess and not the good girls that her parents had raised to represent them in the world.

Wait till you get home to cry. She could wait. She was very good at waiting.

That hour of performing passed, and the girl bowed her head while the preacher prayed for the family before going in for the funeral. They were led to the side anteroom, where four pews provided the grieving family members with privacy. The visitors sat in the sanctuary to hear the eulogy.

The preacher was just right. The Reverend Philip Black knew a few funny stories that reminded grieving people of who Jerry Simpkins had been when in his right mind. He told the stories over the closed casket that contained Jerry's body. "Jerry heard the gospel when he was twenty-one years old, and boy, did it take on him."

The audience tittered appreciatively.

"I remember what my own family thought about Jerry when they first met him. My wife thought he was a fine specimen of a man. Like a movie star. The strongest man she had ever seen, and he could do anything."

The facade began to crumble. The girl who wore my clothes relaxed and settled back. The preacher was telling some truths, and that did a good work in her.

"He was a good businessman and a good father, too. Worked three jobs at one time to support his family."

Our heads began to nod, for he was penetrating our defenses with words of truth — memories that didn't hurt because there was no lie in them.

The preacher shifted his body to look right at us. "You girls may look back on your days with your daddy and have regrets . . ."

"No, we don't," we said in unison, doing the unthinkable. My sisters and I talked back to a preacher when he was speaking from the pulpit.

We turned to each other to say the truth back and forth: "Daddy was loved, and he knew it — maybe not in his mind but in his bones and his blood — till the day he died."

The preacher blinked. "Okay. You girls won't have any regrets, then."

"That's the truth," we all agreed.

My sisters knew the truth. I knew the truth. Daddy had lived the truth. He died, but the truth lived on in us. We had known love together, and we had rightly inferred from that life of love lived out in faith that the Maker of Love is real — as real as life and death.

From the Family Album . . .

Death Takes Its Time

I have not cooked since Daddy died nine days ago. My aversion to the kitchen is not due to the funeral food that came in. Meals arrived, but the size of my hungry family kept the leftovers to a minimum. There aren't any now, and I am tired of eating out, so I've pulled a roast from the freezer and am, in this new way of looking at food, thawing it for supper.

Roast does not particularly appeal to me, but nothing does, so why not cook it? It's already in the house, and I don't want to go to the grocery store. The dinner hour will come, and the gnaw of hunger will commence, but it will not have with it that appetite for something that is supposed to be tasty — for gravy, bread, cake. Mentally I catalog my favorites foods, and I shake my head. I don't want to smell them. I don't want to face the challenge of them on a plate. I don't think I can make my hand and arm operate silverware. And I don't want the heaviness of them in my mouth. I have lost my appetite, and it is probably due to the way that my father's illness affected him just before he died.

At the end of a long journey through Alzheimer's disease, my father lost his ability to swallow. Although my Aunt Eileen had warned me it would happen — and she should know, having nursed her husband for years with the same disease that killed both men — it didn't become real to me until I stood beside my father's bed in the back room where he came to live out his days and where I tried to squirt droplets of water onto his tongue, which was parched dry from breathing hard through his mouth. Even the droplets of liquid I delivered into his mouth as carefully as one anoints an eye with antibiotic medicine could not be ingested without labored coughing. And finally it seemed fruitless — even to me — to punish him by simply trying to alleviate a thirst that could not at that point be quenched.

Instead I sat back on the sofa by his bed in the big back room and did what I had never done before during the long duration of his illness: I did nothing. Out of that helplessness, that inertia, that reaction of a willed passivity to his slipping away from me, I lost my appetite, which has not yet been changed back by the natural rhythm of living — for we go on, don't we? We go on into the flux of daily life so quickly that there is barely time to cast a glance over our shoulder at what once was — at who he was, at who we were with him — because the forward motion of life doesn't easily accommodate the experience of a hard death. And it probably shouldn't.

Mourning is supposed to fit within the prescribed parameters appointed for its expression. But mine has not. At Daddy's bedside, I could not ultimately offer him even a drop of water for comfort. At his funeral, I couldn't cry because he had been released from suffering, and how could I begrudge him that? At the gravesite I stayed dry-eyed once more, and when my sisters watched me covertly to see if I wanted to steal all the flowers from his casket and take them home for the comfort of beauty, I wasn't even tempted. In so many ways I had already been given beauty for ashes, and I didn't need the flowers.

And I don't seem to need food now. I sit in front of food and make my hand move, my mouth work, my throat open up to receive the nourishment, and I think about him, his body fighting death while courting it, and I remember thinking that he looked like a woman in labor who was about to give birth, except it was his soul being born rather than another separate person. Although it was an image that my needy heart may have created, I held onto it, repeated it to people who offered me condolences when all the time I was thinking to myself: *Good-bye, old man. I'll miss you.*

It is this refrain that moves through me instead of an appetite for eating and socializing, although I am a good enough actor to participate in these rituals with others. Most of the people who know me have no idea that I have lost my appetite. I have made all my meetings, have not missed church, and before Dad's funeral I went out and bought two new outfits to wear because I had a will to appear triumphant, as if death held no sting for me. It wasn't pride. It wasn't denial, either. It was a tribute to my father's beauty, his strength. I am not ashamed of that or of the future tears that will come. When they do, perhaps the release will give me back my appetite for food.

But not yet.

I am not in a hurry. In my experience of time, I am still on the sofa in the back room where my Daddy is, and although his death has allowed him to move on, I am waiting out the pace of my own deliverance from this season.

Love has its way with you, and so does death.

The Appraisal

"Can I ask you a few other questions about this house?" Tommy, the house appraiser, asked after he had made his preliminary examination of the property. My sisters and I were getting ready to sell it, and obtaining the appraisal was the first step in the process of placing the house on the market.

I pointed to Mother's kitchen table, and we sat opposite one another.

"Does that fireplace work?" he began, his pen held over his notepad.

"Naw," I replied, sounding like my mother. Her voice popped out of me occasionally, surprising me, for I had not heard her speak in several years now. *Hello, Mama,* my inner spirit muttered — it is that part of me that converses with God and the dead. Some people call it the communion of the saints.

"Daddy changed his mind about having a fireplace after he started building this house. He put one in, but he didn't finish the chimney. Didn't like the idea of a fire burning around us girls. There were four of us." I pointed to our old senior portraits still hanging on the wall, but he didn't turn to look.

Tommy was all business. "This here is a peculiar house, ma'am, and I don't mean that as a criticism."

Feeling mischievous, I asked, "What's peculiar about this house? It's big. It's got lots of bathrooms. It has that nice garage apartment."

"That's not a garage apartment, ma'am," Tommy argued. "That's a den."

"It's an enclosed garage with a bathroom. We've had a small refrigerator and a microwave back there. We girls have been rotating through it. Our daddy was sick."

"It's a den, ma'am."

I let the subject drop and asked, "What about that nice work shed out back?"

"That's what we call an old shack, ma'am. I'm going to credit five hundred dollars in the estimate for it, and that's being generous."

"To some old man or woman that old shack will be worth a lot more," I promised him. My gaze was unwavering. Tommy held it.

"You do have a nice patio and a covered carport. That's worth something. Only you don't use it for cars."

"That's my niece's play area. Katie uses the concrete patio as a large drawing-board. I keep her supplied with colored chalk. My whole family loves beauty. Art runs in the family," I explained, though it didn't seem necessary. Most people have a natural response to beauty. It's one of the reasons we're Christians. How could you have a lifelong love affair with beauty and not also love God?

"I noticed that, ma'am. She's a fine artist. You been parking out front?"

I nodded yes.

"Where is your daddy?" Tommy asked, suddenly looking around.

"Dead," I replied succinctly. I could have offered him the details of Daddy's long illness and sudden death, but Tommy didn't seem to want to know them, and I get tired of telling that particular story because what I am able to say about how Daddy lived and died isn't really the truth: it's just what people are willing to listen to or believe.

Scratching his head, Tommy asked, "Do you know why he built way back here at the back of a subdivision? You're never going to get the value of this house from the sale. It's overbuilt for the area. The only people I feel sorrier for than you are those two schnooks who've just built on those two lots in front of you."

"Really?" I asked, grinning.

"Really," he confirmed.

"Daddy built this house himself with his own hands. He built mine, too. It's down the road a piece past those two poor schnooks."

"No offense."

"None taken."

"It's a solid house. It's just odd. How do people get to the ball field behind it? Do they have to cross your lot to reach it?" Tommy made a clicking sound with his tongue.

"I think they have an entrance off Main Street thataway," I said, pointing behind him. "The city has actually tentatively approached us about buying the two acres behind Daddy's house for a parking lot or a walking trail — I'm not sure which."

Tommy looked like he could cry. "Lady, please don't do that. You chop off that back lot so that a hundred kids and their dogs are running through here, and you'll never get rid of this house."

Actually, I wasn't thinking about selling the land to the city. I was thinking about giving it to them. I liked the idea of kids having a safe place to play with their dogs. "You're telling me unequivocally that the ball field is not a sales feature for this house."

"That's right. The only thing that could make your situation worse is if you're sitting on a flood plain. I'm gonna check, because you're pretty close to the river."

"We are on the flood plain," I assured him brightly.

"Maybe you're not. Maybe you can scoot in under the line. It's gonna be close, though."

I smiled consolingly at him. "Even if we weren't, the Alabama River is only two miles over there. I don't need somebody who marks a map to tell me that if it rains long enough, that river is gonna come this way." I released a sigh and sat back in my chair. "We could all drown any minute." I grinned again.

Tommy eyed me suspiciously, wondering if I suffered from a condition known in the South as having a screw loose. "Are those double-thick window panes?" He gestured to the kitchen windows that framed the view of the back lot.

"Yep, but the seals are broken. That's why the glass is cloudy."

"How about insulation in the ceiling?"

"You can count on it being double what the requirement is. Same for the walls." I had seen Daddy order the extra insulation, watched it being blown in.

Having gotten answers to all of his questions, Tommy straightened his papers and got ready to leave. "I'm going to do the best I can by you on the appraisal, but there are some things about this house . . ."

I interrupted him. "Just write down the truth as you see it. Let your figures represent that."

"Well, I know you want to get as much money as you can for it," Tommy said.

"No, I don't," I said simply. "I only want as much money as it's worth to someone who wants to live here. The buyer ultimately determines the price. You're just making an educated guess about the value so that a lending institution will guarantee a loan."

He smiled. "That's right, ma'am. A lot of people don't know that. I'll have an estimate for you by the latter part of next week." Passing through the kitchen doorway, he slapped the walls and said, "It'll last a long time. It was built solid."

"That's right," I affirmed. "Daddy knew how to build a house."

When he got to the front porch, Tommy stopped and turned, sheepishly admitting that he needed to be paid. He had forgotten to ask for a check. I waved for him to sit down on one of the porch chairs and went back inside for my purse. While I filled in the numbers, he looked out at the woods that separated us from the poor schnooks who had followed in Daddy's pattern of overbuilding at the back of a subdivision on the flood plain.

"Nice view," he said. "I can see how you must have been happy here. Are you in a hurry to sell it?"

"I'm not in a hurry about anything," I replied truthfully.

"Well, that's good, I suppose. I don't know who you're going to find to buy this place," he said.

"I do," I boasted. "Once upon a time, I worked in the advertising department of a newspaper. I shall place a want ad geared to adult children who need a house large enough to accommodate their own family and an aging parent. That garage apartment will come in very handy." Then, I added, eyes squinting, "I don't care what you call it. When I write the ad, I'm calling it a garage apartment."

"I wrote down 'den,'" Tommy asserted.

"That is your prerogative," I allowed. "But I shall write what I think is true." It was not the first time that the responsibility of naming the truth felt like my job.

"I'll have the appraisal sent to you next week," Tommy promised again. The beautiful view held him, and I saw him linger. I know that tension. Beauty is a powerful draw.

"I'll be here," I replied, taking my preferred position in a lawn chair on the front porch. I was in no great hurry to see his figures. For no sheaf of pages with numbers or even other facts on them could do the job of accurately appraising the value of this house our father built.

From the Family Album . . .

Babe in the Woods

We bound across the almost three acres of land on the riding lawn-mower.

"Deeper!" Katie shouts above the roar of the engine. Putting her mouth closer to my ear, my seven-year-old niece growls, "I wanna go into the deep, deep woods."

Gripping her solidly, I nod, and we head toward the dense thicket of bramble and grass that really needs to be bush-hogged. The deeper we go, the more entranced Katie becomes. She loves the land. She leans hard into me, her right arm crooked around my neck, bracing herself with her left leg while she sits on mine.

We mow rough terrain together for an hour. Katie, strong and tall for her age, lifts branches out of our way. She works the blade. She steers when sweat or grit blinds me temporarily, but she doesn't like to do it for too long. There's a point when it occurs to her that she is guiding us, and that moment of realization causes her to turn to me, suddenly wanting me to take over. I do, gripping her tightly, guiding us while her hands imitate mine, poised over the steering wheel. I explain how we mow and why we lift the blade when we pass over roots. She listens carefully, attracted to real work in a way that children and many adults often aren't.

Her vocabulary includes words like "ignition," "carburetor," "flooded," and "David!" For neither of us is so learned that we can do without David Zimmerman, the gentle man who stepped in to help us when my daddy no longer could. But we do as much as we can. Dad died two months ago, and this land his granddaughter and I continue to mow was his — is ours now, temporarily. It's on the market; but before we sell it, I rob death of some of its sting by helping this grandchild, who has an innate relish of what she thinks are deep woods, to understand the labor and commitment involved in making them habitable.

Twenty years ago my daddy cleared this land. He built the family home with his own hands. He built my house beside it. He and I often walked the land together, communing with the beauty of the woods while calling his frequently rambling dogs and examining water-drainage problems. When he got sick, I began to do the work he had always done. Now I swap lawn-mower stories with Harold McGalliard at church, who understands why, if I had it to do again, I'd buy a John Deere instead of this model I selected randomly from Wal-Mart when I was a babe in the woods about the benefits of a wide-cutting swath and more horsepower.

It's too late for that, for I won't need this mower much longer. A big family will come along that wants a spacious, comfortable house with four full bathrooms and this land. I consider how it will feel to turn over Daddy's land and Mama's house to strangers, and whether the next family will take as much pride as Katie and I have in maintaining Daddy's vision for the land — in achieving what our realtor Joan Partridge describes accurately as "a park-like setting."

It is more a park than a woods, but deeper, closer to the creek, the brush is thicker, and there is a tree down from a recent storm, and enough greenery and vines to give a young girl the impression that the job is a big one and that not just anyone can do it. She and I can. I want Katie to know that fulfillment. I want her to be unafraid of dirt and sweat and challenges. I want her to know that muscles are not the ultimate reward of aerobic exercise that allows females to wear spandex and dance to popular music. Working muscles and the experience of accomplishment are powerful, efficient tools, like a quality lawn-mower.

In these days of mowing Daddy's land — of saying good-bye to the past and heading fearlessly into our futures — I want to impart to Katie an understanding that is more valuable than family land. One day when I and her other protectors are no longer here, I want this girl to know from experience that she can confront any terrain, however rough, and make it habitable.

Acknowledgments

M any friends have believed me when I said I couldn't have lunch because I had to work. For their understanding and patience, I sincerely thank Sue Luckey, Jennie Polk, Fern Smith, Lori Tennimon, and Marilee Mallory.

Other friends have encouraged me in so many ways. Heartfelt thanks to Rex Snider, Betty Snider, Elaine Harry, Melanie Muzio, and so many others still at Millbrook Presbyterian Church. I also thank my new friends at Trinity Presbyterian Church: the Berean class and my lunch bunch, particularly Anne Richardson for organizing us. Many preachers have fanned my faith; I recognize and celebrate the spirit of Christ in the Reverends Kirby Smith, Michael Brock, Steve Muzio, Claude McRoberts, Patrick Curles, and my beloved Stanley Hartman and his beautiful wife, Maribeth. Thanks also to the Reverend Philip Black, my daddy's friend.

For occasional legal counsel, I thank my attorney John Thornton. For a faithful readiness to keep my whole family seeing straight, I thank Jack Cates, also a preacher, of Cates Optical. For solving a multitude of problems and then accepting only a cup of coffee for his help, I am deeply grateful to the humble and wonderful David Zimmerman.

For encouragement and abiding friendship, I am indebted to Chancellor Guin Nance of Auburn University at Montgomery, who taught me to write. I also thank Professor Nancy Anderson, a great encourager of writers and presently the mentor for some very precious children who are participating in her writing programs through the AUM-Taulbert Initiative.

Other editors who have encouraged me are Susan Ager, Paul Bernstein, Lary Bloom, Larry Conley, Marcia Lythcott, John Lux, Mary Jane Park, and Margaret Carroll, who saw and first cultivated many of the pieces about Dad for *The Chicago Tribune*. Presently, I am thankful to Cassandra West, who has also edited my columns for *The Chicago Tribune*.

Finally, I am indebted to the ever-patient and always insightful Mary Hietbrink, the editor at Eerdmans who has worked with me and asked just the right question at just the right time and then waited until I found the answers. Thank you, Mary.

My large extended family has also helped me with memories and interest in this story. Much love to Lola Leigh McCord and Jon Linna, Jody Helms, Rhonda and Jody Helms, Jan and Garrick Hrivnak, Ben Helms, Steve McCord, Jerrod McCord, Matthew and Shan McCord, Joe and Marlene Morris, Eileen Hagan, Phyllis and Bob Gibson, Teri Ferrell, Betty Ann Thorne, Judy McCord, Albert Morris, and the daughters of my very dear Uncle Tommy Morris, Elizabeth Morris and Eva Luckie.

Finally, although I have dedicated this book to my sisters, I thank them here for their generosity of spirit in letting me tell this story the best way I could. I have probed their memories while searching mine. Any mistakes are probably just a product of confabulation, which runs in the family.

The Chicago Tribune originally published "Dad Goes Bananas," "Say Good-Bye," and "My Mother's Child."

"The Legacy of a Very Handy Man" first appeared in *The Detroit Free Press*.

The Atlanta Constitution originally published "Can You Hear Me, Brother Woodrow?"